wh... child has...

ADD/ ADHD

✓ Get the Right Diagnosis
✓ Understand Treatment Options
✓ Help Your Child Focus

Rebecca Rutledge, M.D.
Series Editor: Vincent Iannelli, M.D.

Aadamsmedia
Avon, Massachusetts

Published by
Adams Media, an F+W Publications Company
57 Littlefield Street, Avon, MA 02322. U.S.A.
www.adamsmedia.com

Contains material adapted and abridged from *The Everything®
Parent's Guide to Children with ADD/ADHD,* by Linda Sonna, Ph.D.,
copyright © 2005, F+W Publications, Inc.

ISBN 10: 1-59869-666-1
ISBN 13: 978-1-59869-666-0

Printed in Canada.

J I H G F E D C B A

Library of Congress Cataloging-in-Publication Data
is available from the publisher.

This publication is designed to provide accurate and authoritative
information with regard to the subject matter covered. It is sold with
the understanding that the publisher is not engaged in rendering
legal, accounting, or other professional advice. If legal advice or other
expert assistance is required, the services of a competent professional
person should be sought.

—From a *Declaration of Principles* jointly adopted by
a Committee of the American Bar Association
and a Committee of Publishers and Associations

Many of the designations used by manufacturers and sellers to distinguish
their product are claimed as trademarks. Where those designations
appear in this book and Adams Media was aware of a trademark claim,
the designations have been printed with initial capital letters.

*This book is available at quantity discounts for bulk purchases.
For information, please call 1-800-289-0963.*

Contents

Chapter 7: *Anger, Organization, and Worry—Emotional Struggles...95*

Chapter 8: *Dealing with Difficult Behavior...*129

Introduction

Attention-deficit hyperactivity disorder, which is often referred to as either ADHD or ADD, is probably one of the most misunderstood common childhood disorders.

Although ADHD is said to affect about 3 to 5 percent of children, some experts say that it is underdiagnosed and undertreated in many children.

Even with all that is known about ADHD and the increased awareness about this disorder, there are still a lot of negative associations with being diagnosed with and treated for ADHD. Some of this goes back to the days when there were fewer ADHD medicines and so children were left to deal with the side effects of medication, such as weight loss, difficulty sleeping, or feeling like a zombie.

Fortunately, there are now more options and most kids can be treated with the right dosage of the right medication to eliminate or greatly reduce side effects.

Still, there is often a social stigma to being diagnosed with ADHD that keeps some parents from going to their pediatrician. They may even avoid thinking about ADHD when their child is struggling at school and has obvious ADHD symptoms, including hyperactivity, impulsivity, inattention, and getting easily distracted.

Parents also often believe that ADHD medications will lead to later drug abuse or that their kids will learn to use their medicine like a crutch. The opposite is actually true, though. Most studies show an increase in drug abuse in children with ADHD who are untreated. And kids with untreated ADHD are more likely to do poorly in school, have behavior problems, and develop poor self-esteem.

When Your Child Has . . . ADD/ADHD educates parents about the basics of ADHD, how to get an evaluation, and what treatments are available. The information on coping with ADHD symptoms and how they affect family life, anger management, and dealing with difficult behaviors, will be especially helpful for many parents.

Chapter 1

Understand the Basics

10 Things You Will Learn in This Chapter

- How to recognize the first signs of ADD/ADHD in your baby
- The differences between the three types of ADD/ADHD
- The prominent symptoms associated with attention deficit
- The prominent symptoms associated with hyperactivity
- If your child can grow out of it
- About external stimulation and how it affects children with ADD/ADHD
- Why an impulsive child may have difficulty making friends
- How your child's impulsivity can be dangerous
- How to tell if your child has behavioral issues and not ADD/ADHD
- About the criteria for a true diagnosis

Life with Your ADD/ADHD Child

James's father smiled as he watched his small son run in circles around the coffee table. "He certainly is all boy, isn't he?" he asked his wife. His wife frowned. She wondered if all little boys were such bundles of energy. Her friends said their toddlers had acted like little perpetual motion machines at his age, so maybe James's behavior was normal and he would outgrow it. Still, she thought it strange that he showed no signs of tiring after running for ten minutes as fast as his legs could carry him. Actually, he was running faster than his legs could carry him. "Slow down, honey," his mother said. James gave no sign of having heard her. A moment later he tripped and fell. His head hit the coffee table and made an alarming thud.

DOES THIS SOUND LIKE YOUR CHILD?

Hyperactivity and problems getting babies to pay attention typically appear when they begin to crawl and walk. Because normal tots are so active, inattentive, and impulsive, making this sort of diagnosis is a difficult and complex process.

Learning from a Mistake

James's mother kissed his latest boo-boo. "You need to be careful," she said. But as soon as his wails subsided, he was off and running again. He widened his circle and spread chaos throughout the house as his mother trailed after him, issuing no-no's. When she turned her back, he pulled an entire row of books off the shelf. While she was putting them away, he dumped out his toy box and scattered blocks across the room. While she was picking up the toys, he somehow scaled the dining room hutch and emptied an entire drawer. If she sent him to his room for a timeout, he would wreak havoc there, too.

James's mother put on a video and bribed him with a snack to sit down and watch. Even while his eyes were glued to the screen, he continued to fidget and squirm. It was as if James was in his own zone, and he couldn't seem to stop himself even if he wanted.

Current Definitions

The Diagnostic and Statistical Manual of Mental Disorders, Fourth Edition, Text Revision (*DSM-IV-TR*), which was published by the American Psychiatric Association in 2000, lists all of the mental and behavioral disorders currently recognized by U.S. doctors. The standard attention-deficit/hyperactivity disorder diagnosis is divided into three types. The "predominantly inattentive type" is for children with attention deficits but no problems with hyperactivity. The "predominantly hyperactive/impulsive type" diagnosis is used for hyperactive children, who may also be impulsive. The "combined type" is for children with both inattentive and hyperactive/impulsive behaviors.

DID YOU KNOW?

According to the U.S. Centers for Disease Control and Prevention, 78 percent of school-age children, or 4.4 million in the United States, ages four to seventeen years, have ADD/ADHD.

Can You Wait and See if Your Child Will Grow Out of It?

Adolescents and adults may outgrow or overcome their symptoms. If so, they are diagnosed as being "in partial remission." However, rather than reflecting a cure, this reflects the new view that people do not outgrow the disorder but may learn to compensate so that the symptoms are not disabling. There is also a catch-all diagnosis for children who don't meet the standard criteria. If they don't have enough symptoms or their symptoms aren't severe enough, they can be diagnosed with an atypical form of ADHD called "attention-deficit/hyperactivity disorder not otherwise specified" or ADHD-NOS.

But Aren't Toddlers Normally Active?

Of course, toddlers naturally tend to be active, impulsive, and inattentive. What makes the diagnosis of ADHD so problematic lies in the ability to distinguish between "normal" toddler behavior and what falls outside that range. Keep in mind that children with ADHD display extremes in these behaviors and often appear to have no self-control over them. Be on the lookout for behaviors that cause significant problems in your child's day-to-day functioning. If you are unsure whether what you're observing is normal, there are specialists who can help. We'll take a look at that further later on, but for the meantime, do not feel as if there is no support out there for you and your child.

Predominantly Inattentive Type Attention Deficit

Take a look at the following symptoms. As you review them, you will begin to see why it is hard to differentiate "normal" from "problematic":

- Difficulties listening, even when being directly addressed.
- Difficulties continuing to pay attention to activities involving either work or play.
- Difficulties paying attention to details and avoiding careless mistakes.
- Difficulties completing tasks, chores, and assignments.
- Difficulties organizing activities and tasks.
- Difficulties doing tasks that require sustained mental effort, like that required for schoolwork.
- Difficulties keeping track of possessions and materials, such as toys, clothes, homework papers, and school supplies.
- Being easily distracted.
- Difficulties remembering.

In order to be considered bona fide symptoms, it should be clear that a child cannot sustain attention and cannot concentrate on age-appropriate mental tasks for extended periods. Problems stemming from boredom, disinterest, lack of motivation, and defiance are not supposed to be counted as ADD symptoms—though they often are. It is easy to see why attention deficits create problems in school. Students with short attention spans cannot concentrate on schoolwork for long periods as is required to do their work. Being easily distracted poses a major problem in crowded classrooms, which are filled with continuous rustles and murmurs. If students' attention wanders at unpredictable moments, they miss portions of lectures and don't hear explanations about assignments and tests.

DOES THIS SOUND LIKE YOUR CHILD?

Combine all of the ADD symptoms, and what emerges is a description of an absentminded professor. If your child has his head in the clouds and can't keep his feet on the ground, an ivory tower might be just what the doctor ordered. When he's scaled the academic heights, losing mittens and wearing mismatched socks won't seem like such major problems.

Frustration for You

Lapses of attention when a parent gives directions and instructions can result in considerable frustration and upset at home. A parent might send a child to clean up his room and later discover him playing with baseball cards instead of doing his chore. If the child's attention strayed while the parent was giving instructions, the youngster might have understood that he was to go to his room but missed what he was expected to do when he arrived. Or, after going to his room to clean it, he might see his box of baseball cards and spend an hour going through them without giving another thought to what he was supposed to do.

Organizational Nightmares

If your child is a disaster when it comes to his organizational skills, first consider his level of development. Research shows us that a child's intellectual, spatial, organizational, and emotional abilities can develop at varying rates. Just because your child may seem to be quite bright for his age, the part of his brain that handles organizational tasks may be slower to come along. Thus it makes sense that parents are often bewildered by a child's seemingly high level of intelligence while he can't keep anything together! So before the diagnosis of ADD is made, this is an important matter to consider.

With that said, poor organizational skills can cause a host of problems in school and at home. Many children get confused during projects and tasks to the point that they don't know how to proceed. Some youngsters become upset and cry over seemingly simple homework assignments and chores, claiming they don't know how to do them. If parents and teachers are convinced that a youngster is bright enough and possesses the skills needed to do the work, they may conclude that the child is overly emotional. Other youngsters don tough-guy masks and display an "I couldn't care less" attitude, so it is hard for adults to recognize that poor organization is at the heart of many of their problems. The solution may be to break long assignments and projects into a number of small steps and have students complete them one at a time.

Poor organization can also lead children to make many careless mistakes when completing assignments and chores. Unless students are methodical and focused while doing schoolwork and checking their answers, they may end up overlooking some items altogether. They misnumber problems so that all of their answers are counted as errors or make many small mistakes that lower their grades. Again, if carelessness stems from indifference, laziness, or an unwillingness to put forth the effort required to line up numbers and check work, the problem should not be considered a symptom of ADD.

What Is Hyperactivity?

The second type of attention-deficit/hyperactivity disorder, which includes hyperactivity and impulsiveness, is technically known as the "predominantly hyperactive type." Most people refer to it simply as ADHD. For this type, children's difficulties must stem from hyperactivity or from a combination of hyperactive and impulsive behaviors. Altogether, the DSM-IV lists six symptoms of hyperactive behavior and three symptoms of impulsive behavior. A child must have six out of the nine symptoms to be diagnosed with the predominantly hyperactive type.

Symptoms of Hyperactivity

Hyperactive children have an excessive energy level. They are described as appearing to be driven by a motor, so that they continue to wiggle even when at rest:

- Squirming and fidgeting even when seated
- Getting up when expected to remain seated
- Running excessively and climbing in inappropriate situations
- Difficulty playing quietly
- Being always on the go
- Talking excessively

Some youngsters squirm and fidget while sitting at their school desks, while watching television at home, and while listening to bedtime stories. Hyperactive adolescents may swing their legs, tap their feet, drum their fingers on their desk, pop their chewing gum, or chew their fingernails. Some teenagers keep getting up from their desks to wander through the classroom, run through the house, or climb every tall object in sight. They are more likely to report that they feel restless much of the time. Some say that when they must remain seated for more than a few minutes, they feel as though they're about to jump out of their skin.

Just because a parent or teacher says a child's level of activity is excessive, this does not always make it true. Some parents cannot tolerate a lot of activity around them. Teachers often have too many children to control, so a child who seems more active than normal can be very frustrating. Again, please remember that you are looking for an activity level that interferes with your child's ability to join in other activities, sit quietly when necessary, and to learn.

Too Little or Too Much Stimulation

Despite their short attention spans and inability to pay attention in school, they can concentrate on a video game or television program so well that they don't even notice when someone is standing two feet away, yelling for their attention. Most parents find this extremely irritating. They think their child is defiant, pointing out that he concentrates and sits still well enough "when he wants to."

Actually, the words "attention deficit" are somewhat of a misnomer when we look at these children. In fact, their brains are being bombarded with so much information that they are unable to filter out what is the important information to pay attention to. It's as if their brains are like an overloaded circuit board. Thus they often end up paying attention to nothing!

And yet, in order for their brains to be able to focus, professionals believe that some kids require much more stimulation to remain attentive than the average youngster. As anyone who has sat through a long sermon or attempted to read a book they find boring knows, the mind must have enough stimulation to remain attentive. If there is too little, the mind begins to wander. The natural physical response is to become fidgety and restless, as if the mind were trying to create some additional stimulation in order to stay awake. When children diagnosed with ADD and ADHD are fully engaged in a highly stimulating activity such as a television program or interactive game, they become so attentive that they cannot readily shift their attention away from it. Do the minds of children diagnosed with ADD/ADHD move at the same speed as a fast-action video game and rock video? This seems to be a possibility.

Impulsiveness

In addition to hyperactive behavior, children diagnosed with ADHD may also behave impulsively. Impulsive children have difficulty inhibiting the urge to act or speak and often seem unable to contain themselves. There are three main signs doctors look for:

1. Blurting answers before the teacher or parent has finished asking the question
2. Not waiting his or her turn
3. Interrupting conversations or intruding into other's activities

Impulsive children reach for fragile objects despite repeated reminders not to touch. They grab other children's toys without asking permission. At school, they get up to sharpen their pencils the moment they determine their tip is dull or broken without waiting to ask permission. Parents and teachers spend a good deal of time and effort admonishing impulsive youngsters to slow down and think before they do or say something, but they seem incapable of remembering. Many parents come to doubt the intelligence of children who don't anticipate the consequences of their actions. But for those diagnosed with ADHD, the problem is not lack of intelligence or willful misbehavior. Their minds simply work differently.

DOES THIS SOUND LIKE YOUR CHILD?

Peers dislike having other students disrupt the classroom, interrupt their conversations, and intrude in their games, so impulsive children often have social difficulties. Some impulsive children alienate others because they have hair-trigger tempers and are quick to take affront.

The knee-jerk reactions of impulsive children may occur because they are actually wired differently. Scientists hypothesize that the part of the brain controlling automatic reactions propels them to react before the part that handles conscious thought can process and evaluate information.

Symptoms and Diagnosis

Although every child could qualify for a diagnosis of atypical ADD/ADHD, the requirements for a standard ADD or ADHD diagnosis are quite stringent. Besides having enough symptoms of attention deficits, hyperactivity, and/or impulsiveness, signs of these problems must have been present early in childhood—at least before age seven. While a child might not have been evaluated by a professional until after that age, the developmental history must indicate that the behaviors were present early in life. In addition, the current troublesome behaviors must have been present for at least six months. Behavior problems that have been going on for shorter periods are more likely to be reactions to a specific trauma or life change, such as the birth of a sibling or a family move. To be considered symptoms of ADD or ADHD, the behaviors in question must be more frequent and disruptive for the child's day-to-day functioning than is typical for youngsters at the same level of development. Children must have serious behavioral problems in two or more important settings for a standard ADD/ADHD diagnosis:

- At home
- In school
- With peers
- On the playground
- At work

Where Is the Most Problematic Place?

Behavior problems that are limited to home are more likely to stem from family stress, poor parenting, or difficult family dynamics. If students have problems at school but get along well in other environments, this usually suggests they are struggling with teaching or learning difficulties.

Only having problems getting along with peers is usually due to poor social skills. Problems that are confined to the playground, including unsupervised playtime in the neighborhood, suggest problems coping with unstructured situations or having a personality trait known as risk-taking or thrill-seeking. People with this trait require more stimulation to avoid boredom, and they are drawn to activities that most youngsters would view as overly dangerous or frightening.

DOES THIS SOUND LIKE YOUR CHILD?

Ask yourself this: Are these problems present across the board in your child's life? Does she keep getting in trouble at school? Could she have ADHD? Well, if she is doing well in other settings, the first step is to find out if there is a problem at school that needs attention. Everything from being bullied to having an especially strict or permissive teacher can cause children to act up. Sit in the classroom to observe.

Problems getting along at work can develop when children are old enough to hold down jobs. If teenagers are having difficulties at work but get along in other settings, there's a good chance that simply changing jobs or employers will solve the problem. Hence, a standard ADD/ADHD diagnosis should not be made when a child only has significant problems in one setting.

How "Clear" Is Your Evidence?

In addition to having serious difficulties managing in several environments, the standard attention-deficit/hyperactivity disorder diagnosis requires "clear evidence" of "significant impairment in social, academic, or occupational functioning," according to the *DSM-IV-TR*. Impaired social functioning might mean that the child cannot make or keep friends because of his offputting behavior. The way to determine that a child's academic functioning is impaired is to compare scores on standardized achievement tests with IQ test scores. If achievement test scores are much lower, it is important to look more deeply into whether there is a learning disability. In fact, large percentages of children with ADD/ADHD also have coexisting learning disabilities. On the other hand, compromised test scores may just be due to the fact that your child wasn't trying that hard on testing day or that he performs better on tests that are structured differently.

Another issue to consider is whether there is a family history of ADD/ADHD. In fact, genetics accounts for about 80 percent of the causes of ADD/ADHD. There does seem to be a genetic predisposition to having ADD/ADHD at birth if one or more close family members (a parent, sibling) have it.

DID YOU KNOW?

A child with a low energy level can be diagnosed with atypical ADD/ADHD. So can a daydreamer. In fact, a youngster with any combination of problematic behaviors can be diagnosed with atypical ADD/ADHD. The technical name is attention-deficit/hyperactivity disorder not otherwise specified (ADD/ADHD-NOS).

There are also some questionnaires that can be used to pinpoint symptoms and that will aid in the diagnosis. A good diagnosis should be derived from several sources: your observations, teachers' experiences with your child, a medical opinion, and testing (if possible). The more information you can collect about your child, the more accurate the diagnosis is likely to be.

Is There Such a Thing as a Standard Diagnosis?

For the standard (as opposed to "atypical") ADD/ADHD diagnosis, a child must have many specific symptoms reflecting difficulties with attention, hyperactivity, and impulsivity. In addition, the problems must have started before age seven, and they must be pervasive, and severe. However, a child can be diagnosed with attention-deficit/hyperactivity disorder not otherwise specified (ADHD-NOS) with just a few symptoms that only create problems in one setting and that started later in life. The *DSM-IV-TR* indicates that this diagnosis is even appropriate for children with "a behavioral pattern marked by sluggishness, daydreaming, and hyperactivity" or low energy level. Any combination of problematic behaviors can now be diagnosed as ADD or ADHD.

Does Your Child Meet the Criteria?

Few experts now believe it is necessary for all of the criteria to be met before ADD/ADHD is diagnosed. Since academic success is so important for a child's current and future happiness and well-being, most doctors diagnose and treat it even if the behavior problems only occur at school. Be that as it may, it really does not make sense to say that symptoms must have been present early in life. Hyperactivity and inattention can stem from head injuries or lead poisoning that happens after age seven.

Is There an Upside?

Unfortunately, because it is called a disorder, the positive aspects of ADD/ADHD can be easily overlooked. Kids with ADD/ADHD are often:

- Highly intelligent
- Intuitive
- Energetic
- Creative
- Curious
- Adventuresome
- Contagiously enthusiastic

When a parent forgets to consider the positive aspects of ADD/ADHD, they begin to see a child as more of a problem than a joy. Being afflicted with ADD/ADHD does not have to be a bad thing—it is simply a neurological disorder that will require attention (pardon the pun!). Having ADD/ADHD does not have to predispose your child to a lifetime of trouble and unhappiness unless you let it!

Chapter 2

Evaluations and Results

10 Things You Will Learn in This Chapter

- Who is qualified to diagnose your child—and who is not!

- About legislation that works to discourage overmedication

- About medical tests that correspond with psychological evaluations

- What happens in a parental interview

- The behavioral checklist and how it will help determine a diagnosis

- How testing is different for younger and older children

- About educational and intelligence testing and the connection to ADD/ADHD

- How learning disabilities affect many children with ADD/ADHD

- Whether or not you need a second (or third) opinion

- How looking deeper into your child's symptoms can save him/her in the long run

Qualified Professionals and the Right Diagnosis

Today, anyone and everyone seems to feel qualified to diagnose ADD/ADHD. Relatives, friends, and even grocery store clerks offer opinions about rowdy youngsters, suggesting that they are hyperactive or have an attention deficit. School-aged children do the same, referring to disruptive classmates as "hyper." It may appear that almost anyone can recognize ADD/ADHD symptoms and make a diagnosis in a matter of moments. But resist the urge to take a layperson's opinion. The diagnosis should never be made merely because a child is active or disruptive.

Teacher Evaluations

Classroom teachers are usually the first to urge parents to seek an ADD/ADHD evaluation. Because they work with so many students, teachers have a better basis than parents for judging whether behavior is typical. Because teachers are less emotionally involved, they also tend to be more objective than parents. If a teacher says that a child has ADD/ADHD and needs to be treated, parents usually respond by scheduling a doctor's appointment immediately. But many teachers are anxious to eliminate behavior problems and think that medication is fine if it makes the class easier to manage. And most parents do not realize that some doctors consider a teacher's report of problems and recommendations sufficient to warrant an ADD/ADHD diagnosis and to write a prescription as a sort of "quick fix." This is a dangerous practice.

▰▰▰ DID YOU KNOW?

Many children with ADD/ADHD have learning disabilities. Therefore, a thorough educational evaluation is often a good idea if you or a teacher sus-
pects this sort of problem.

Qualified Diagnosticians

The first place to look for help in determining
whether your child has ADD/ADHD is to contact your
child's pediatrician. Although this may not be a spe-
cialty area for your pediatrician, he is almost always well
versed in ADD and ADHD symptoms. If he feels he is
unable to make a definitive diagnosis, he is likely to refer
you to the second most popular source for diagnosis—a
psychologist. Any state-licensed psychologist can legally
diagnose and treat ADD/ADHD. Psychologists special-
ize in psychological testing and in treatment. They do
not prescribe medication in most states, although this
limitation is changing.

Although it isn't always necessary, psychiatrists can
make the diagnosis and prescribe medicine if it is warranted. Licensed educational counselors can also diagnose disorders and make treatment recommendations
if they have a doctorate degree, but they do not usually
provide treatment.

Other professionals may be able to help diagnose
children based on your child's specific issues and problems. These may include:

- Neurologist
- Audiologist

- Allergist
- Clinical nutritionist (licensed by the Clinical Nutrition Certification Board)

Medical Tests

There are no traditional medical tests to diagnose ADD/ADHD. Pediatricians often use questionnaires designed to pinpoint particular clusters of symptoms. Psychologists also use these measures as well as some more objective tests such as IQ testing to make sense out of what they have observed in a child.

DID YOU KNOW?

Kids with other disorders or medical problems can mimic ADD/ADHD. These include vitamin deficiencies, thyroid problems, allergies, and even middle ear infections. A thorough medical examination is always recommended.

Along with other routine medical tests, children should be tested for allergies and sensitivities, since they produce symptoms that are routinely mistaken for ADD/ADHD. Children should have their hearing checked. Middle ear infections can be so minor that there is no fever, but the combination of muffled sounds and feeling under the weather can make children distracted, inattentive, and irritable. An audiologist should investigate the possibility of language processing problems. More testing means less guessing and more answers—if you can afford these tests and think they might be helpful, it can't hurt to investigate.

Evaluation Methods

Methods of evaluating children for ADD/ADHD are not as scientific as most people assume. In fact, they are not scientific at all. Because children's behavior typically improves in unfamiliar environments such as waiting rooms and examining offices, doctors do not expect to personally witness the behavior problems that are of concern. So many rely on information provided by a parent or teacher.

Parent Interviews

The typical first step in the evaluation process is to collect background information and take a detailed developmental history. The goal is to ascertain the exact nature of the behavior problems; determine that they have been present for at least six months; establish that they occur in multiple settings; identify any special stresses the child has been under; find out what has been done at school and at home to try to help; and ensure that another diagnosis does not better explain the difficulties. To prepare for the interview, collect your youngster's medical and school records and take them with you to the appointment unless your doctor requests them in advance. If you have recorded information in a baby book about the age at which your child first sat up alone, walked, talked, etc., be sure to have it with you as well.

The parent interview usually takes about an hour. Some physicians spend only fifteen to thirty minutes obtaining basic information about the problems and then refer the child to a psychologist or psychiatrist to take the developmental history, screen the child for emotional problems, and determine whether other psychological and educational testing is needed.

Behavior Checklists

These are the questionnaires that provide a checklist of problem behaviors for a parent to complete, and a similar checklist is sent to the child's teachers so they can indicate which they have observed. Often the checklists are mailed to the school before the first appointment so the doctor can review the information in advance. If teachers do not respond, most doctors attempt to talk to them on the telephone. Although parents and teachers tend to report different problems on the behavior checklists, they usually agree that the youngster's behavior is difficult, trying, and frustrating.

Necessary Companion Tests

It may be necessary to screen for other emotional and mental disorders before a diagnosis is made. Depression, anxiety, and stress reactions from psychological trauma ("posttraumatic stress disorder") cause difficulties with sustaining attention and produce agitation that can look so much like hyperactivity, even seasoned professionals cannot tell them apart. Moreover, about one-third of children diagnosed with ADD/ADHD have one or more coexisting disorders. Some pediatricians, family practice doctors, internists, and neurologists regularly perform mental status evaluations, so they have a good deal of solid experience screening youngsters for mental health problems. But if your family physician is uncomfortable making a diagnosis of ADD/ADHD, he is likely to refer young patients to a child psychologist or psychiatrist rather than trying to conduct this type of screening himself.

▶ DID YOU KNOW?

Adolescents should be screened for alcohol and drug use before psychotropic medication is prescribed since the combination can be lethal. A 2001 Department of Health and Human Services survey found that 19 percent of teens consumed five drinks during a single sitting in the previous month.

Observing Children Is the First Step

If mental health screening suggests that a youngster has another psychological problem in addition to or instead of ADD/ADHD, further evaluation by a psychologist, psychiatrist, or another credentialed mental health provider is in order. A routine psychological evaluation involves taking a psychosocial history by interviewing parents in order to identify current and past individual, family, and social problems. Trauma from parental divorce, abandonment, alcoholism, abuse, domestic violence, and stress from chronic family tension can cause ADD/ADHD symptoms and other psychological, behavioral, and learning problems. Older children are then interviewed at length and younger children are observed in a playroom. Children age six to twelve typically undergo a combination of interviews and playroom observations.

The Need for Further Evaluations

If the interviews and observations suggest a need for further evaluation, the next step is likely to be psychological testing. In a perfect world, a complete psychological evaluation would include personality, intelligence, neuropsychological, and educational testing. A school psychologist or educational diagnostician employed by the school district may be legally obligated to administer some or even all of the tests, which relieves the family of this financial burden. However, if you cannot afford all this testing, it's perfectly appropriate to ask what testing is *absolutely* vital for your child's particular set of problems.

DID YOU KNOW?

A test to measure how quickly and accurately a child responds to images flashed on a computer screen can be used to assess impulsiveness. However, this test is usually administered in laboratories during research investigations and is rarely used in clinical settings.

Educational Testing

It would be great if all children diagnosed with ADD/ADHD could undergo educational and intelligence testing to rule out all sorts of problems. But it is hard to get that done unless the child is really having a lot of problems or isn't responding to medication.

Because learning disabilities are rampant among children with ADD/ADHD, there is a good chance that special education services will be helpful. Moreover, students with severe learning problems often misbehave in school or simply stop paying attention because they are frustrated and overwhelmed by the work. They act up at home because they are upset about their inability to succeed academically. Their ADD/ADHD symptoms disappear once they receive instruction targeted to their particular learning style and needs. The same applies to students who are especially academically advanced, except that their inattention, frustration, and classroom behavior problems are more likely to stem from boredom. They settle down and their concentration improves when they are given more challenging work. Educational testing can often pinpoint issues that are causing children to misbehave.

Should You Get a Second Opinion?

Three-year-old Valerie's behavior improved dramatically when she took the medication the pediatrician had prescribed. When the doctor was checking her during a followup appointment, her mother asked how long she would need to keep taking it. "Most likely through adolescence," the doctor replied, "Quite possibly for the rest of her life." When he saw Angelica's shocked expression, he added, "ADD/ADHD is inherited. This is not something she is likely to outgrow."

After Angelica learned about the many things that could cause Valerie's type of behavior problems, she took her to a psychologist for an evaluation. The psychologist determined that Valerie was missing her father, whom she saw infrequently. Since the deterioration in her behavior coincided with the family breakup and move, he believed that diagnosing her with ADD/ADHD had been an error.

Looking Deeper

The psychologist also expressed concern about her daycare center. He talked to Valerie's teacher on the phone and heard some disturbing conversations in the background. "The workers sounded impatient and were yelling at the children and ordering them around. Valerie may order other children around because she is copying their behavior. In any case, children her age must be taught how to get along with peers. Punishment makes some youngsters more aggressive without teaching them what to do." The psychologist recommended moving Valerie to a different daycare center, increasing visitation with her father, and having a child psychiatrist evaluate her need for medication. The psychologist personally thought that grief counseling would probably make medication unnecessary. If those measures were not enough, he would recommend additional testing to rule out other medical problems. That made much more sense to Angelica than medicating Valerie for years on end.

Chapter 3

ADD Details

10 Things You Will Learn in This Chapter

- Why it seems like your child never listens
- How children with ADD are supersensitive to sounds, temperature, tastes, etc.
- Why it's very important for you to offer support and admiration
- About ADD symptoms and a connection to fetal alcohol syndrome
- How the teenage years can be the toughest of all and why
- How some serious psychiatric disorders are linked to highly creative people and why
- Why some children strive for perfection and others lose interest
- How schedules are a huge challenge for some children to follow
- Why students with ADD might struggle through elementary and high school and excel in college
- How to discuss difficult issues with your child—and get him or her to listen!

Challenges Your Child Will Face

When many adults read about attention-deficit disorder (ADD), most recognize that they had all the symptoms when they were growing up. Some eventually learned to compensate for or even overcome some of the problems that made childhood so challenging for them. However, many still have great difficulty with a number of tasks that come naturally to most people. As adults they feel freer to be themselves, either because they surround themselves with like-minded people or because they have stopped caring about what others think. Still, many successful adults carry the scars from their difficult childhoods.

DID YOU KNOW?

Only after their children are diagnosed and have begun treatment for ADD do they realize that they too might be suffering from the disorder. When looking at your family history, don't overlook yourself just because you were never diagnosed as a child.

Educating the ADD Child

Children with ADD struggle in traditional classrooms and are commonly viewed by their teachers as unintelligent or as underachievers. Many come to think of themselves as not very bright or unmotivated. The real problem is that their minds work differently from most people. They are more holistic in their thinking and are drawn to abstract ideas rather than details.

Because they focus on the "wrong" parts of the lessons or they may not focus on the lessons at all, they can easily forget, mix up, or simply overlook information that teachers consider important.

Spending Mental Energy

Many are accused of being lazy because they daydream. Often the real "problem" is that they devote a lot of mental energy to pondering the material being presented rather than simply trying to commit it to memory. They consider its relationship to other things they have learned and contemplate its implications. Often these children are more intuitive, so when asked what they are thinking about, they may be unable to articulate what is on their mind. If they try, they are often ridiculed by teachers and peers who cannot comprehend the connection between their comments and the subject under discussion. Thus they end up being accused of not listening or of not paying attention— and are diagnosed with ADD.

DOES THIS SOUND LIKE YOUR CHILD?

Highly sensitive children react strongly to sounds, temperature changes, smells, and tastes that others barely notice. Such acute sensitivity goes hand in hand with artistic, musical, and literary genius. Do not assume your child is exaggerating when he complains about discomforts that to you seem minor.

Peer Problems

Many kids with ADD "feel" they are very different from their peers, and the majority do not understand how they think or why they behave as they do. Peers tend to regard them as strange or odd because of their unusual interests. Especially creative types are often branded as crazy because their heightened sensitivity causes them to have stronger emotional reactions than less sensitive people. Even if these children do find a social niche later in high school, they know that most of their peers regard them as odd. Some children are very independent and do not notice or care how others perceive them, but many notice and they care a lot.

Support Your ADD Child Early On

Feeling lonely, rejected, and being viewed as strange during childhood can cause long-term difficulties with self-esteem. Without their parents' support, many youngsters find themselves without anyone to affirm them as people. Their desperation often propels them toward an antisocial peer group. Others label themselves as crazy and withdraw. Some hold everyone at a distance for fear of having their "insanity" discovered. When children with ADD are not accepted by their peers, affirmation from parents becomes all the more important.

Parent Problems

Most people pride themselves on being practical and realistic. They focus on the details of everyday life, accept things at face value, and rarely pause to contemplate abstract matters. They prefer the tried and true to the unknown and uncertain. They devote a lot of energy to trying to arrange the present in order to ensure that the future does not hold too many surprises. They value conformity and are disturbed by independent thinkers who are not careful about adhering to social conventions. Parents may appreciate the artistic, literary, and scientific contributions of creative people and admire their inventiveness and creative problem-solving abilities. But they urge their children to follow the beaten path and make decisions about important issues such as courses of study, careers, and mates based on their heads. Most people consider the heart less trustworthy.

➤ DID YOU KNOW?

Some ADD symptoms can stem from impaired brain functioning due to fetal alcohol syndrome, lead poisoning, allergies, chemical sensitivities, or another brain trauma or injury. However, the ADD symptom list also describes the personality of most highly creative individuals.

Growing Up with ADD

Good family support is probably more important for ADD children because they suffer more peer rejection and find it harder to please their teachers. Youngsters who achieve success in their chosen field often say that their warm family relationships were critical sources of emotional support. Their parents might not have understood what made them tick. But their families

encouraged them to develop in their own direction
instead of adding to the pressure to conform. Having
a supportive parent seems to make for a much happier
childhood, but some children received critical emotional support from a teacher, relative, or neighbor who
believed in them. That can enable them to maintain
feelings of self-worth.

A BETTER PARENTING PRACTICE

Please Understand Me by David Keirsey and Marilyn Bates and *Nurture by Nature* by Paul and Barbara Tieger describe the special strengths of different personality types. They should be required
reading for parents who are having difficulties
understanding their child. Put them on your must-
read list!

Special Difficulties for Adolescents

Struggles to define a personally fulfilling identity
typically intensify during adolescence. Feistier teenagers
commonly distance themselves from parents who dis-
count their goals, deride their ambitions, and strive to
change them. The results are often alienation and family rifts. Compliant teens may let their parents' dictates
override their own wishes and pursue college majors and
careers their parents consider practical. That can result
in poor grades, dropping out of school, or worse: pur-
suing unfulfilling careers and marrying someone whose
main appeal is that their family approves. Too often,
such children end up with serious regrets decades later.

Complex Ideas and Problems

ADD children who are highly creative enjoy complex ideas and problems. Routine tasks that do not pose an appealing intellectual challenge try their patience, and repetitive tasks set their teeth on edge. Sorting and putting away clean clothes, doing pages of handwriting practice, or completing dozens of simple arithmetic problems strikes many as too mindless to be of interest. When they finish, they do not feel pride in their accomplishment because it seems meaningless. Praise for a job well done may not motivate them if the job seems mundane. They may prefer to toss all of their socks into a drawer even though they must spend a lot of time rummaging through it each morning to find two that match. This seems nonsensical to people who find organizing easy and enjoy having things in order.

DID YOU KNOW?

Scientists believe that highly creative people are genetically inclined toward serious psychiatric disorders, especially depression, manic-depression, and substance abuse. In addition, peer rejection and years of feeling like failures at school and disappointments to their parents predispose children to psychological problems. Be supportive!

Many creative children never learn to write legibly because they cannot bring themselves to do page after page of handwriting practice. Like Einstein, many highly intelligent creative youngsters are very adept at comprehending complex concepts and developing new ones, but they are abysmal at performing simple computations, which require rote memorization. At the same time, tasks that seem to others to involve boring, repetitive practice may strike creative children as fascinating. Young pianists practice scales on the piano for hours because perfecting them poses a challenge.

Method to the Madness

ADD children can appear to be hopelessly disorganized, but often there is a method to their seeming madness. They use inventive methods to break the monotony of routine tasks to stave off boredom and remain alert and focused. For instance, they skip around when doing sets of problems for assignments and tests instead of doing them in order. They experiment with different problem-solving strategies instead of finding one that works and sticking to it. In the process, they overlook some problems altogether and make errors that do not seem to follow a pattern. Their uneven performance confuses educators, making such students ripe for a diagnosis of a learning disability.

DOES THIS SOUND LIKE YOUR CHILD?

Many creative children are mystified by adult reverence for the calendar and clock. Teachers refuse to accept late work, believing that when students do their lessons matters more than that they do them. Some children march to a different drummer because they keep time to their internal rhythms.

Life in the Here-and-Now

It is hard to generalize about children who are by nature nonconformists, but many do share certain characteristics. One is that many have great difficulty adhering to schedules. In part, that is because dividing time into slots and assigning activities to each one does not strike them as sensible. If they worry about being late, it may be because they are afraid others will be upset. They do not believe that the passage of time is significant or that the clock should rule people's lives. Many are doers, not planners. The future and past matter less to them than the present. In that, they are in accord with the world's philosophers who teach that the only reality is the here and now. Overly anxious creative youngsters may obsess about the future or ruminate about the past. However, the issue is more likely to be that they do not know how to identify or manage the anxiety they are feeling at the moment.

Seeing the Forest, Not the Trees

If your child is highly creative and has ADD, she will typically have a holistic thinking style. Because she focuses on how things merge, combine, and connect, she is able to see the big picture. Indeed, the ability of creative children to analyze and synthesize ideas while ignoring details can be mystifying. They do not automatically focus on the elements that define subtle differences, which are required to sort and organize. Teachers commonly see academic failure on the horizon. A matching or true/false test that requires students to recall specific information about Civil War generals and battles is likely to be very challenging. Yet their ability to expound on the strategies used in various military campaigns on an essay test may be very intelligent and incisive. Teachers warn that students cannot succeed academically without getting the details straight. However, if these youngsters do not give up and drop out altogether, they are likely to find college not only more gratifying but actually easier than elementary and high school. Many do not begin to shine until graduate school where original, creative thought is highly prized.

DID YOU KNOW?

ADD kids need to learn to organize their possessions and cope with schedules, since these skills are important for school and most job settings. Most children are eager to learn, but staying organized requires an attention to niggling details they do not normally focus on.

Parents often worry about how their child with ADD symptoms will manage a job and a household because she is so haphazard about details. In fact, many go on to be very successful adults. They develop impressive new theories, produce spectacular inventions, and create dazzling works of art, music, and literature that enrich the world and contribute to its betterment. They may also lose their keys every time they turn around and forget to get their driver's license renewed. Many have to make repeat trips to the grocery store because they keep forgetting things. They do not bother with grocery lists because they know they will lose them. Yet they survive. And those who pursue careers that utilize their special talents thrive. They make fine parents despite being exceptionally messy housekeepers.

With all of that said, it is probably hard for you as a parent to look that far ahead. Your child is having problems now, and you shouldn't underestimate how difficult that is for him and for you.

Your Role in All of This

Some children are very independent from the time they are tots, and this can be true for kids with ADD who are intellectually gifted. Individualists often clash with their teachers even though they are not disruptive. Some read books in class instead of doing busy work assignments. Some draw instead of sitting with their hands folded on their desks. Some create complex stories in their imaginations to fend off boredom. They persist because what they are doing interests them very much. Parents' and teachers' negative opinions are less compelling than their desire to learn. Some believe the only ways to get them to change may be to use heavy-handed punishments to break their spirits or to medicate them, but this is not always true.

DOES THIS SOUND LIKE YOUR CHILD?

ADD kids can become so engrossed in what they are doing, they do not notice what is going on around them. If they do notice, they may not care to join in. Getting them to care may be a losing battle.

Many ADD children tend to be outspoken. They are prone to address adults like equals rather than deferring to their authority. If they are generally insensitive to other people's feelings, they may alienate peers and earn a reputation among adults for being ill-mannered. Maintaining good relationships with teachers and classmates can be especially challenging for those who love to debate. Some children consider ideas more important than people's feelings.

Discussing All This with Your Child

Help your child understand how his behavior effects others. It is a mistake to take your youngster's side against teachers, but it is also a mistake to try to change your child into someone he is not. A better approach is to communicate in no uncertain terms that you expect your child to be respectful of others. Discuss ways he can assert himself appropriately. And when he hurts someone's feelings, he of course needs to apologize.

DID YOU KNOW?

The social and emotional cost of being different is high, and many parents work hard to get their youngster to act like the other children. During adolescence, the desire to conform and act like peers can lead to trouble. Be careful what you wish for!

Fitting in with the Group

Students are expected to participate as members of the class and move with the group even during recess and lunch. If they also attend after school programs and extracurricular activities, they have little time to ponder their own thoughts or pursue their individual interests. Highly intelligent and creative students are not content to soak up bits of information so they can spit them back on a test. Moreover, some are not very adept at memorizing facts and remembering specific details. Nevertheless, they may be masterful when it comes to grasping concepts. But some need to conduct their own investigations and draw their own conclusions. They have a hard time making sense of material that is presented to them orally or in writing. Having an unorthodox method of processing information does not mean they are deficient. It does, however, mean that they are different. And being different is definitely difficult.

Every Child Is Different

Studies have shown that the brains of children diagnosed with ADD function differently. Because they tend to be in the minority, it can be very hard for the majority to comprehend—much less appreciate—values, attitudes, and ways of being in the world so different from their own. Sometimes it helps the majority to understand how their own personality characteristics limit them.

To Be Organized or Not to Be Organized

Have you ever noticed how very organized people work hard to keep their ducks lined up in a row? Unfortunately, the world around them is inherently unpredictable and chaotic. Rather than forcing your ADD child to be as organized as you are, you may do well to learn to tolerate some level of disorder instead. As a result, you will be more open to solutions that will actually work with your child and his limitations. If your child is extremely disorganized, you will notice that he is having problems keeping track of his belongings, finishing his tasks, and even enjoying other activities. Your job then becomes helping him to develop techniques that work for him, and not necessarily for you. Remember, the world is going to expect some level of organizational ability from your child, so preparing him for that will be immensely beneficial.

Shades of Gray

While most people can readily manage black and white issues, they have a tendency to become immobilized when confronted with many shades of gray. Remember, ADD kids are already finding themselves overloaded with information. As they become increasingly bombarded, they will postpone decisions until they get more details and information, even though it is obvious they will never get enough. They will abandon projects simply to avoid the ambiguity of many situations.

It is important for you to help your ADD child to become comfortable taking risks. When she says, "I have always done it this way," or "Everybody else does it this way," try another approach. Help her to understand that the old ways of doing things may not always mean that it ever worked well or that the majority was right.

A BETTER PARENTING PRACTICE

In order to enjoy your disorganized child more, you may do well to make yourself more flexible, tolerant of chaos, and less concerned about details and schedules. The key, however, lies in helping your child find her own ways of coping such that she can maneuver herself in the "real" world.

Find a way to appreciate the differences in the way your child organizes her world and how she solves problems. She may even have techniques that can actually work for you, too. Take those abilities and find a way to "tailor" your rules and expectations to your child's specific strengths and weaknesses.

Chapter 4

ADHD Details

10 Things You Will Learn in This Chapter

- How the vocabulary of ADHD has changed through the years

- About the redefinition of the disorder and how it now affects millions of children

- How exercise can change your child's life

- Why you want to control what your child pays attention to—but can't!

- How some symptoms of ADHD can be an asset

- Why so many more boys are diagnosed than girls

- The difference between "thrill-seekers" and children with ADHD

- How traditional classrooms are very limiting for some students

- That spankings rarely instill a sense of punishment for children with ADHD

- How children with ADHD can grow up to be hard-working citizens and which jobs suit them the best

A Special Challenge for You
Frederick was diagnosed with ADHD at age five. At age twelve, his mother was as distressed as ever by his daredevil behavior. He ran into the street without pausing to look for cars and zoomed about on his skateboard as though he had a death wish. The only time he settled down was to play video games, and then he would not let go of the joystick when it was time to go somewhere or do something else. Frederick was finally having a good year in school. His mother thought it was because he had a male teacher who would not put up with his nonsense. Sometimes people complimented her on having such a polite, well-behaved son. "If only you knew him like I did," she would sigh. She wished someone understood what she had to put up with.

DID YOU KNOW?
If your child seems to have problems behaving in only one particular area—such as school or home—the problem may not be ADHD. If he shows control in one venue, then he ought to be able to control himself in others. A diagnosis of ADHD would not be warranted in this case.

Frederick was going to spend the entire summer with his aunt and uncle. They were so strict that they made their kids study an hour every day during the summer. If nothing else, that should convince Frederick how easy he had it at home! When his mother called to check on him, her sister said that she was not giving Frederick his medication, but he was behaving "beautifully." Her brother-in-law echoed her comments. "He's welcome at our house anytime," he said. Frederick's mother could not imagine what their secret might be. Or had he been misdiagnosed?

When Does Active Turn to Hyperactive?

In generations past, hyperkinesis was the diagnosis for children whose motor activity was so constant and intense, their bodies seemed to vibrate, and their hands shook when they tried to write or play with a small toy. Their activity was markedly unfocused, so they could not complete short, simple projects even when they were highly motivated. Playing meant wildly rummaging through a toy box or drawer as they searched for the toy they wanted, then impulsively dumping the contents onto the floor because they could not instantly find it. No sooner had they spotted what they were looking for than a sound would float in from another room and they impulsively raced off to investigate. Most children actually were suffering from a serious medical problem such as epilepsy, mental retardation, cerebral palsy, or brain damage.

■■■■ DID YOU KNOW?

Children with a "sensory-perceiving" temperament are action-oriented with a fun-loving zest for life. Too often, they are misdiagnosed as having ADHD. They have much to teach the more serious, sedate majority about the joy of living in the moment. Read *Please Understand Me* by Keirsey and Bates to learn more.

New Definition Means More Diagnosis

Now the term hyperkinesis has been changed to ADHD and the definition has been expanded. Children are being diagnosed by the millions, including an estimated 10 percent of boys! The vast majority would have been viewed as normal in other times, and their behavior is considered typical by parents from other cultures. Some veteran child therapists say they have rarely seen a youngster who is totally physically unable to control his activity level.

AN INTERESTING FINDING

One research investigation that looked at assessing ADHD found that nearly two-thirds of parents subjectively rated their hemophiliac child (hemophilia is a rare blood disorder) as inattentive, hyperactive, or both.

Realistic Expectations

Is hyperactivity only in the eyes of the beholder? It may seem so because the differentiation between mere activity and hyperactivity can be a very subjective experience, and again, you must look for activity that causes problems for your child in his day-to-day functioning. When a child cannot sit still long enough to learn or to enjoy certain activities on a regular basis, hyperactivity may be the culprit.

Even a brief bout of mild rowdiness can upset parents terribly. A minor lapse of attention is major when bumping into something could prove life-threatening. But rowdy behavior is normal and is not dangerous for healthy children. Because it involves vigorous physical movement, it is good for them. Expecting children to behave like somber adults is unrealistic!

Dealing with Symptoms

Symptoms of ADHD are lots of fidgeting and restlessness. Yet, a lot of either or both do not mean that a child is out of control; they mean that she is bored and needs to get some exercise. While exercise will not cure the hyperactivity in ADHD, it is extremely beneficial to help these kids let off steam. Recommend somersaults, jump rope, hitting a tennis ball against the side of the house, or going for a walk. At least suggest that your child stand up and stretch for a moment.

➤ A BETTER PARENTING PRACTICE

To help your child tolerate being able to sit still, encourage "breaks" that allow your child to get up and move. Switching from an activity to a break from it may well help to keep boredom at bay.

Encourage Exercise!

Lack of exercise is seriously compromising the health of American children. The symptoms include obesity, high cholesterol, high blood pressure, diabetes, and behavior problems. For many students, gym is their only chance to move about, but many schools have cut back so that students only attend a few times a week. Even if they go every day, they average only nine minutes of exercise. The rest of the time is spent watching others or listening to the teacher. A study by U.S. International University and reported in Thomas Armstrong's *The Myth of the A.D.D. Child* found that exercise had positive effects on behavior. Hyperactive, aggressive students participating in jumping or field exercises forty minutes a day, three times a week were less aggressive on the days they ran than on the days they did not! Even as parents bemoan the fact that their children get too little exercise, they chastise them for failing to sit still. Parents should be glad they are moving, even if they are only swinging their legs and wiggling in their chairs!

Controling What Your Child Pays Attention To

When your child has ADHD, he still probably has difficulties with shifting attention and in the alternative, being able to concentrate so intensely as to be oblivious to everything else on the other. Parents and teachers find these behaviors frustrating because they want to control them. That is reasonable when the goal is to get them to pay attention during six class periods a day, assuming they have a break between each subject. But expecting these youngsters to sit still and to attend to what others consider important every waking moment is expecting too much.

Shifting Attention Appropriately

Most doctors attribute youngsters' difficulties sustaining attention on the one hand and shifting attention appropriately on the other to a genetic defect. However, if these behaviors are genetic, they do not necessarily signal a defect! Consider this, in hunter/gatherer societies, forests were filled with dangerous animals. Survival depended on being aware of and responsive to each small movement and sound that might signal the presence of a dangerous predator. When hunters spotted game, they then needed to be able to hone in on it during lengthy pursuits without becoming distracted by small movements and sounds.

A Boy Disorder?

ADHD is almost exclusively a young male disorder, with the ratio of boys to girls running about six to one. The International Narcotics Control Board estimated that in 1995, 10 to 12 percent of all U.S. boys ages six to fourteen were diagnosed with ADHD. Girls are more likely to be diagnosed with ADHD Inattentive Type. Yet, when it comes to hyperactivity and impulsiveness, boys still get the lion's share of the labels, the seats in special education classrooms, and the Ritalin prescriptions. Boys also get the majority of the learning disability and conduct disorder diagnoses. The big question is why.

Do You Have a Thrill-Seeking Son?

Children with a personality trait known as "thrill-seeking" are commonly diagnosed as hyperactive. While most youngsters are content to read adventure stories, thrill-seekers need the excitement of the adventure itself to achieve the same emotional high. They concentrate well when they are immersed in an intensely stimulating activity and have great trouble sustaining attention when nothing much is going on. They are perfect candidates for an ADD/ADHD diagnosis.

Understanding Thrill-Seekers

Thrill-seekers find boredom especially noxious and are happiest when the stereo is blasting, the television is blaring, the strobe lights are flashing, and everything is happening at once. Whether they arrived on earth with their minds preprogrammed by genetics or were reprogrammed by television and video games is unclear. For whatever reason, their brains do not register strong reactions to the routine and familiar. Boredom occurs when there is insufficient stimulation and the brain must struggle to keep from falling asleep. It is believed that they are drawn to excitement because they do not derive pleasure from tranquil activities. The fact that they are drawn to danger the way a bookworm is drawn to books puts them at high risk for more than their fair share of injuries.

DID YOU KNOW?

If you don't think thrill-seekers care about getting hurt, you're wrong! They do care but they have a higher tolerance for pain too. Trying to squelch their determination to pursue risk and danger is apt to be a losing battle. They may be terribly accident prone and very athletic at the same time.

Thrill-Seekers in the Classroom

Traditional classrooms hold little appeal for thrill-seekers, since opportunities to do things they find even mildly stimulating are so limited. Many cook up trouble to generate some excitement. They may not even consider trips to the principal's office or the many punishments their parents inflict all that unpleasant. Talking does not make much of an impression. Spankings may not have much effect, either. Parents have to hit so hard to have an impact, those who use physical punishments are at risk for abusing their youngster. Timeouts and being grounded are more motivating, but to avoid defiance and rebellion, keep them short. Although thrill-seekers are not interested in what the rest of the world thinks of them, you can cause much damage by harping on their flaws and failings.

When Do Drugs Help?

Dosing these youngsters with stimulant medications will likely settle them down, but their personalities are going to still be there. In other words, your thrill-seeking child will still be a thrill seeker! Although there is no research on the subject, some experts believe that medicating ADHD may actually postpone serious problems rather than prevent them.

Many young adolescents refuse to continue taking any sort of medication when they are old enough to just say no. Some try to use the excuse with ADHD medicines that they want to feel fully alive and do not want their senses dulled with medication. Interestingly, many teens later gravitate toward stimulants, especially cigarettes, amphetamines, and cocaine.

Protecting Thrill-Seekers

Deterring thrill-seekers from danger is likely to prove impossible. Trying usually fails and alienates them in the process. Parents are better off working to keep them safe while allowing them to be who they are. Try these tactics:

- Buy a skateboard and every type of protective pad on the market.
- Buy a sturdy bike that can withstand a lot of wheelies and leaps, and be prepared to replace it often. Be rigid about requiring your youngster to wear a helmet.
- Channel rowdiness at the swimming pool by providing diving lessons.
- To deter fights, try karate lessons.
- If the choice is between your teen's music and having the entire family go deaf, buy headphones and insist that he use them.

Keep Them Busy

Maintaining solid relationships with thrill-seekers and finding enough pro-social activities to keep them busy is critical for getting them through their teenage years unscathed. And that is no easy task. Their penchant for danger and desire to live on the edge can get them into serious trouble. Their dislike of academics and of being confined puts them at risk for dropping out. Thrill-seekers do not usually aspire to college and do not think in terms of long-term goals. Their aim is to live the present moment to its fullest. Many parents alienate them by trying to get them to forget today and think about tomorrow. Yet indulging in what gives them pleasure often leads to a spectacular outcome. If guitar playing or track turns them on, they may keep playing or running for the sheer joy of it and become accomplished musicians or athletes in the process.

A BETTER PARENTING PRACTICE

If your youngster prefers activities involving physical risk and danger, find some appropriate, yet exciting, activities to grab his interest and sign him up! What he learns about fun during childhood may be how he seeks thrills as an adolescent.

The allure of exciting peers often proves irresistible, so maintaining a positive relationship is critical. Rather than pressing your teen toward college, look for ways to make his life more fulfilling right now. Since high school courses that teach rock music and racecar driving are not offered, vocational classes in machine shop, automobile repair, and carpentry may satisfy him. If you can get him through high school, he may eventually want to go to college. If not, do not despair. Trade schools and apprenticeship programs are options. If he likes large engine repair or a building trade, both pay well. Brighter, more motivated workers often end up managing or owning businesses.

Job Possibilities

In general, anything that involves action and an element of risk tends to be appealing: police officer, firefighter, war correspondent, security professional, forest ranger, military officer, stuntman, rodeo rider, ski instructor, lifeguard, animal trainer, nature guide, machinist, heavy equipment operator. If your child can tolerate a lot of advanced academic study—and many do go to college after they have been out of school for a few years—he may want to major in oceanography to work with sharks, geology to study volcanoes, or forensic medicine to piece together crimes. As thrill-seekers mature, many find satisfaction in mental risks and become entrepreneurs, financial investors, or criminal defense attorneys. Stressful jobs that wear others down may rev their psychic engines.

Finding What Works

When Frederick's mother arrived to see what her sister and brother-in-law were doing that caused her son to behave during his visit, he was playing softball with his cousins out front. Frederick's aunt stepped out to greet her and told the children it would soon be time for dinner. "We're not hungry. Can't we eat later?" one of the children asked. "I don't mind cold food," another called. Frederick said, "Maybe I can do the dishes instead of setting the table." His mother was amazed. His aunt explained, "We would rather that the kids exercise. No need to eat if they're not hungry—assuming they don't mind cold food." The adults ate, and when the children arrived they sat together at the table to chat. Frederick's uncle explained. "We think it's important to sit down together as a family, but we don't always eat at the same time."

▶ DID YOU KNOW?

Thrill-seekers are not very good candidates for traditional therapy, but they can benefit by communicating through toys in a therapy playroom, over checkers in a counseling office, or while shooting baskets with their psychologist.

When Frederick tried to argue about why he did not need a bath, his aunt said, "You played outside. You're dirty. You must bathe." Frederick yelled, "I hate baths!" His aunt replied, "Yes, I know" as she walked away. She explained to Frederick's mother, "He does not have to like baths, but he does have to take them."

Rules *are* important, and children with ADD/ADHD especially need structure and a clear understanding of what is expected of them. Resist comparing your child and your parenting with others, particularly if those kids don't have ADD/ADHD. Find what you need to do to address *your* child's specific needs. Make your own rules and don't worry about how everyone else is doing it.

Chapter 5

Medication and Other Treatment Options

10 Things You Will Learn in This Chapter

- Is medication absolutely necessary?
- How and why amphetamines make some people "speed" and slow others down
- Why combining treatments are most effective
- Which medication is right for your child's specific symptoms
- Why the FDA classifies Ritalin and amphetamines as substances with "extremely high potential for abuse and dependency"
- How to discuss the need for medication to your child
- Parenting skills
- Teaching self-monitoring skills
- To encourage your child to make friends and avoid social stigma
- Statements that your child can use to defend himself against bullies

The Pros and Cons of Medication

Many parents struggle with the debate whether to medicate their children with ADD/ADHD. Will it harm their growth? Will it de-emphasize the need for them to learn self-control? Will it make things worse?

The Pros

If a child with ADD/ADHD is having signs of anxiety, depression, or mood swings, medication may help balance his moods and decrease impulsivity. The child will be able to think more clearly because thought processes are slowed down enough so that he isn't required to try and filter out all of that overwhelming information flooding into his brain!

Concentration and the ability to listen and retain information will improve. Excessive activity will be curtailed and behavior will be more controlled. He will be able to follow instructions and finish activities. He will have a much better tolerance for frustration.

The Cons

It should be said that not all ADD/ADHD kids need medication. It depends on how severe the symptoms are and how much their symptoms are disrupting their day-to-day functioning. The most common side effects are loss of appetite, insomnia, very dry mouth, and jitteriness.

If you are looking for solid information regarding medication and whether this should be an option for your child, you may want to check out the *ADHD Parents*

Medication Guide, cosponsored by the American Academy of Child and Adolescent Psychiatry and the American Psychiatric Association. It also provides information about nondrug options.

The Right Evaluation

Remember the first step in treating your child is to get him evaluated by a professional. If all goes well, the quality of that evaluation will be topnotch. However, due to time constraints, sometimes a diagnosis made by physicians and pediatricians is completed in a single thirty-minute appointment. In that case, you might consider a second opinion. While medication may be an accurate prescription for your child, there may be other options to try first.

The Checkups Are Important!

If medication is a chosen method for treatment, you may have to take your child to the doctor pretty frequently until the optimal dosage is achieved. Once that is done, brief medication checks are usually scheduled every three months for a time, then scheduled at six-month intervals. How long the medications will be used depend on your child's symptoms and your doctor's opinion.

Some medications require constant monitoring for specific complications, such as reduced liver functioning. Like most medications, problems with prescriptions are possible.

DID YOU KNOW?

Most pharmacies store patient records in computers that are programmed to issue alerts when a
patient is taking a combination of drugs that might
interact. That is a compelling reason to fill all your
child's prescriptions at the same store.

Prescribing medication without first conducting a
thorough psychological evaluation is not a good idea.
While some family doctors and pediatricians are trained
to treat patients with serious mental health problems
and are well informed about psychotropic medications,
most are not. A thorough psychological evaluation is
imperative, because the most commonly prescribed
ADD/ADHD medications can make some psychiatric
problems worse and are believed to trigger more serious
mental disorders in susceptible children. For instance,
Tourette's syndrome, tic disorder, psychosis, and bipolar
disorder should be ruled out before stimulant medication can be safely taken.

How Young Is Too Young?

There has been plenty of controversy about the
appropriate age to begin treating an ADD/ADHD
child with medication. A study done by the National
Institute of Mental Health, the Preschool ADHD Treatment Study, released some preliminary results in 2006.
This was the first long-term study designed to evaluate
the effectiveness of treating preschoolers with ADHD
with behavioral therapy and then, in some cases, with
a stimulant called methylphenidate (Ritalin, Metadate,

and Concerta). In the first stage, 303 preschoolers with severe ADHD between the ages of three and five, along with their parents, participated in a ten-week behavioral therapy course. For one-third of the children, ADHD symptoms improved so dramatically that they did not ever proceed to the medication phase of the study.

The other two-thirds of the children in the study were given low doses of methylphenidate with great results. Interestingly, lower doses actually worked better than the doses typically prescribed to elementary students. This is thought to be due to the fact that younger children are more sensitive to the side effects of these medications so less is definitely better when it comes to dosing preschoolers! Incidentally, 11 percent of the children had to stop taking medicine due to severe side effects.

The Truth about Amphetamines

Since amphetamines stimulate the nervous system and make normal people "speed," it seemed obvious that such drugs would cause hyperactive children to start bouncing off the walls and make it even harder for those with attention deficits to concentrate. Instead, it was discovered that amphetamines had the opposite effect: hyperactive children settled down and children with attention deficits became more focused. In the past, it was common practice for doctors to confirm a questionable ADD/ADHD diagnosis by prescribing medications containing amphetamine, methamphetamine, or methylphenidate to young patients. If they settled down and their concentration improved, that was viewed as proof that they in fact had ADD/ADHD. However, now doctors discourage a trial of medication believing that many kids may do a little better on a stimulant, whether they have ADD/ADHD, a learning disability, etc.

Although amphetamines and their chemical cousins make some people feel jittery and nervous, they boost almost everyone's concentration enough so that they can sit still and remain focused for long periods. That is why high school and college students often misuse these drugs.

Nonetheless, according to the American Academy of Pediatrics (*Clinical Practice Guideline: Treatment of the School-Aged Child with Attention Deficit/Hyperactivity Disorder*), almost all studies comparing stimulants alone with behavioral therapy indicate a much stronger effect from stimulants than from behavioral therapy.

Facts about Stimulants
While taking psychostimulants, disruptive behaviors decrease dramatically and attentiveness improves for most children. The effectiveness of stimulant medication tends to decrease over time, and studies of long-term use have generally been disappointing. Initial improvements in behavior and grades are not followed by significant long-term improvements on achievement tests. Psychostimulants appear to be more beneficial when combined with educational interventions, psychological treatment (especially cognitive-behavioral

therapy), and parent counseling. In 2002, children received 11 million prescriptions for psychostimulants. Types of stimulants include:

- Ritalin, Metadate, and Concerta (methylphenidate)
- Adderall, Adderall XR (dextroamphet-amine and amphetamine), and Dexedrine (dextroamphetamine)
- Cylert (pemoline)
- Focaline XR
- Strattera
- Daytrana
- Vyvanse

What Are the Differences?
If you look at the drug information pamphlets provided with any prescription, you will be bombarded with facts about the drug and you will probably notice a very long list of side effects. The FDA requires that drug companies list every single side effect reported when a particular drug has been taken. While it is perfectly appropriate and well advised to look over the information included, don't overreact and decide you shouldn't let your child take a medication based simply on that list of side effects. Your best bet is to talk with your prescribing physician and inquire about the most widely reported side effects. Also ask what side effects may pertain to your child's unique makeup.

Ritalin, Metadate, and Concerta

Although these drugs are related to amphetamines, they are not the same. These stimulants increase the activity of chemicals called dopamine and nonadrenaline in areas of the brain that play a part in controlling attention and behavior. It has been successfully used in smaller doses with children under the age of six.

The major side effects for these drugs are sleeplessness and dizziness, while a smaller percentage may experience slowed growth. If any of these drugs are prescribed to your child and you see no improvement in his symptoms, it may be wise to talk to your physician about discontinuing them and trying something else.

Adderall, Adderall XR, and Dexedrine

Adderall, Adderall XR, and Dexedrine are some of the most popularly prescribed stimulants today to help control behavior, attention, and impulsiveness. The "XR" in Adderall means "extended release." It contains ingredients that allow a child to have to take the medicine only once a day rather than having to remember a second dose during the middle of his day. It is not recommended for children under the age of six. Although it is generally very well tolerated, the most reported symptoms include a loss of appetite, insomnia, emotional lability, depression, and stomachaches.

Again, do not be necessarily disturbed over the list of side effects. Just be aware of them and watch to see if these appear in your child and do not stop.

Cylert

Structurally in terms of its chemical composition, Cylert is similar to methylphenidate. It is believed to produce a very noticeable decrease in symptoms rather quickly, which is a great benefit for children. However, if no observable changes of symptoms have occurred within three weeks, talk to your physician. It is recommended for children over six years of age.

The largest concern about Cylert has been the report of liver damage. Since its marketing in 1975, fifteen cases of liver failure have been reported. While this may seem like a small amount, the rate of reporting ranges from four to seventeen times the rate expected in the general population. This estimate may be conservative because of under reporting and the amount of time that has passed since the beginning of an individual's treatment with the drug such that there is a limited recognition of the association. That means the risk could actually be higher.

With that said, Cylert may have been perfectly fine for your child, but it was discontinued in 2005, so is no longer used.

Focalin XR

Focalin is a newer drug in the treatment of ADHD and thought to be quite safe with some of the same side effects as Ritalin. It has been indicated for children over the age of six, so pay attention if your child is under that age and your physician recommends a trial.

Strattera

The active ingredient in Strattera works to increase the levels of a natural chemical called noradrenaline. Noradrenaline is involved in passing messages between brain cells so it plays an important role in regulating attention, impulsiveness, and activity levels. Again, it is considered safe for children over six. Side effects include drowsiness, loss of appetite, mood lability, and irritability. Suicidal thoughts and attempts have been associated with this drug, but again, let your physician be the judge as to whether this is an appropriate drug for your child. Strattera was the first nonstimulant that could be used to treat children with ADHD.

Daytrana

This is an interesting drug because it comes in the form of a patch. It is a clear, flexible, and discreet form of methylphenidate or Ritalin. Daytrana may be a good fit for children who don't like taking pills. Prescribed for children over the age of six, side effects are generally mild to moderate.

Vyvanse

Vyvanse is an exciting development because one dose can last up to twelve hours with significant effectiveness. It is prescribed for kids over six years of age.

A BETTER PARENTING PRACTICE

Keep track of your child's stimulant medication! Many middle school and high school students boost their allowances by selling off their pills. In a Massachusetts Department of Public Health survey, 13 percent of high school students and 4 percent of middle school students admitted to illicit use of Ritalin.

When the Drugs Wear Off

In the "crash" as the drugs wear off, it is common for children to become more aggressive than they were to begin with. (This has led to the stereotype of the violent adult "speed freak" that is in the throes of withdrawal.) Some children become more depressed than aggressive when they "crash." This is less common with the development of drugs such as once-a-day medicines like Daytrana and Vyvanse.

Periods of abstinence or "drug holidays" have been considered. For example, if a child is not in school, such as the weekend or over the summer, kids are allowed to go drug-free. It has also been thought to be helpful in combating some of the harmful long-term side effects, especially on growth. On days that Ritalin is not taken and when the prescription is stopped altogether, the production of growth hormone increases, as if the body is trying to make up for lost time. Drug holidays are a less prescribed practice now because there are so many ADHD drugs available that do not need or require a period of abstinence.

DID YOU KNOW?

Some doctors put an inordinate amount of faith in stimulant medications. If ADD/ADHD symptoms worsen or do not improve, they conclude that the problem is more serious. A poor response to a medication does not mean something else is wrong!

Potential for Growth

It is hard to tell whether children who take stimulants for several years eventually reach their growth potential or not—who can tell how tall they would have become if they had not taken them? Using a growth chart and seeing if your child is following his particular growth curve and is close to his genetic potential for his predicted height can help you monitor any problems. One study found that youngsters who had a lot of problems with nausea and vomiting during their first year on Ritalin ended up a bit shorter in height even though they had drug holidays. Their adult height was compared to children who never took Ritalin, as well as to children who took it but did not have a lot of digestive side effects.

Side Effects on Children's Brains Too?

Peter Breggin, psychiatrist and the author of *Talking Back to Ritalin*, suggests that long-term adverse effects on the brain may be significant as well. Many doctors assume that once the most prominent effects of stimulant medication have worn off, which happens in a matter of hours, the child returns to normal.

In truth, even after stimulant medication can no longer be detected in the system, a youngster may not return to normal for quite some time, according to Breggin. He cites studies suggesting that changes in the brain can linger for months, even though only a few doses were taken. After longer periods of regular use, brain scans have shown shrinkage in certain areas of the brain. This might occur because Ritalin decreases blood flow to the brain.

Alternative Methods

Many parents just can't face the idea of putting their children on medication. The tricky part about these alternatives is that many are not controlled by medical agencies that monitor effectiveness, side effects, etc. It's as if, for the most part, parents are "on their own" when it comes to making decisions about these treatments.

Natural Supplements

Fish oil and other nutritional or herbal supplements have been mentioned as alternatives that are effective for treating symptoms of ADHD. They are said to reduce anxiety and promote healthy functioning of the brain.

Because there is such a wide selection of these alternative remedies, choosing which ones to try is a daunting process. Also, there is no standardization in the industry of herbal medicine, so there is no guarantee to the consistency and the potency of the products you purchase. If you decide to go the natural route, it is still important to discuss this with your child's physician. Many stores that offer these products also have experts who can answer questions. In any case, even if your physician is against your decision to use these remedies, keep him informed.

Other parents swear by limiting certain foods, such as caffeine and sugar, to decrease symptoms of ADHD. While there is certainly nothing wrong with adjusting your child's diet, this alone is not going to get rid of all the ADHD symptoms.

Cognitive and Behavioral Techniques

Some parents swear by a program called *AttenGo*. This is a revolutionary, clinically proven program that uses innovative neurocognitive training online. Results have shown dramatic improvement in:

- Attention
- Concentration
- Focus and memory loss
- Learning disabilities
- Central auditory processing disorder
- Sensory integration dysfunction
- Cognitive impairment related to injury and aging

Behavioral therapy is almost always prescribed either alone or along with medication. This sort of therapy involves teaching both the child and the parent techniques for handling symptoms. An example would be helping the child develop skills for learning to sit still, managing his emotions, and controlling his impulsiveness. Part of the reason behind behavioral therapy is to help a child understand that while his disorder is a problem rooted within the brain, medication should not be considered the answer to managing all of his symptoms. These are techniques that can help him compensate for his symptoms. Most experts agree that a combination of behavioral therapy and medication is the most popular and effective treatment for ADHD.

Dealing with Social Stigma

Lots of students refuse to take medication at school and are horrified by the prospect of having their peers discover that they are taking it. At home being told they are acting "hyper" is a criticism, and being similarly criticized by peers seems too humiliating. But peers do not necessarily use the term hyper derogatorily. It depends on the context and tone of voice. Many students say, "I'm hyper," or "He's hyper," as straightforwardly as if they were saying, "I'm in fifth grade," or "He's a hockey player."

DOES THIS SOUND LIKE YOUR CHILD?

A sensitive or defensive youngster may overreact to comments about taking medication. Help your child understand that the intent may not be to upset him. If that is in fact the goal, he needs to find out what an attacker is mad about and not get sidetracked by name-calling.

There is a big difference between teasing and harassment. Students aren't usually harassed because they have been seen standing in line at the nurse's office. They are more likely to be targeted due to their disruptive classroom behavior and inappropriate interactions on the playground. Some youngsters are able to improve their standing in the social pecking order once their symptoms are under control and they are less disruptive. Popular children with good self-esteem use humor to diffuse tension, or they respond assertively to let others know that insulting, demeaning treatment is unacceptable. Aggressive responses tend to alienate others and make matters worse. You can help your child devise ways to turn enemies into friends—or at least, to stop harassment—by roleplaying at home. Consider the following:

PROVOCATION: "I think you need another pill. You're acting hyper."

Aggressive Responses

Technique:	*Trade insults*
Response:	"Look who's talking, four-eyes."
Typical Reaction:	Hostilities escalate
Technique:	*Challenge*
Response:	"Oh yeah? So what are you going to do about it?"
Typical Reaction:	Fight
Technique:	*Bully*
Response:	"Maybe you wouldn't say that if you were missing a few teeth."
Typical Reaction:	Fight; or back down and retaliate later

Technique:	*Retaliation*
Response:	(Pushes antagonist later in the day while passing in the hall)
Typical Reaction:	Alienates his antagonist as well as peers who witness the provocation and do not know the background

Technique:	*Tattling*
Response:	"I'm telling on you."
Typical Reaction:	Teased about being a tattletale; however, reports to the principal may get results

Assertive Responses

Technique:	*Humor*
Response:	"You want to see hyper?" (twirls in circles like a whirling dervish)
Typical Reaction:	Laughter; tension diffused

Technique:	*Sarcasm*
Response:	"I am shocked to hear such rudeness from a good kid. Get up on the wrong side of the bed? Try the other side. It can work wonders."
Typical Reaction:	Embarrassed smile

Technique:	*Self-disclosure*
Response:	"You wouldn't want someone teasing you about being over-weight. Let's drop the insults, Okay? I'd rather play."
Typical Reaction:	Backs down
Technique:	*Find allies and stand together*
Response:	"Last week you picked on Wesley, now me. We don't like it and want it stopped. You're welcome to play with us if you can behave."
Typical Reaction:	Bullies eventually learn to keep a distance
Technique:	*Identify the problem as a first step toward solving it*
Response:	"If you can't say what you're mad about straight out, maybe we need a mediator."
Typical Reaction:	"What's a mediator?" Tensions may subside during the ensuing conversation

Teaching Your Child to Deal with the Stigma

Even if children never use the humorous comebacks they invent while roleplaying, laughter can help them gain a better perspective. Children often reject paren-tal suggestions for handling peer conflicts because they sound too "dumb" or "dorky." Usually that means the comments sound too adult. Try to help your youngster understand that although some bullies rule by brute force, most leaders rise to power because they are more mature than their peers—or at least more verbal. Saying, "Maybe we need a mediator" to a bully may draw derisive hoots on the playground, but onlookers are likely to be a bit impressed as well. That can translate into heightened respect.

A Valuable Lesson

When discussing ways to resolve peer conflicts, emphasize the importance of not backing an opponent into a corner. Otherwise, he may feel compelled to fight to save face even if he would rather forget the whole problem. A back door should be left open so an antagonist can save face while retreating. At the same time, the front door should be left open to create the possibility of future friendship. To that end, a child can say, "You're welcome to play with me if . . . " or "Why don't we just play and talk about this some other time?" Comments like, "Okay. So I'm sorry already. What are you going to do about it?" stir the proverbial pot. "Okay. So I'm sorry, already. Can we please just get on with the game?" can move a relationship forward.

Chapter 6

ADD/ADHD and Your Family Life

10 Things You Will Learn in This Chapter

- How disruptiveness and chaos can abound in an ADHD family

- Why ADHD kids may need more attention

- To determine what it is that your family really needs

- How to enjoy extracurricular activities with your child without yelling, fighting, or getting frustrated

- How watching TV can affect a child's performance in school

- How your child's diet may affect his symptoms of ADD/ADHD

- How cooking dinner together can be fun and capture your little one's attention

- Ideas for family weekend activities that encourage togetherness

- How to turn mundane chores into learning experiences with your child

- That making little sacrifices for your child can truly make a difference in his development

A Different Kind of Life

Don's parents both worked long hours, and to say that
their days were hectic was putting it mildly. They knew
their family was not unique. Everyone else seemed to
struggle with the same frenzied schedule. But other
people's children did not have ADD/ADHD. It never
occurred to them that their lifestyle might be exacerbat-
ing his symptoms.

The Daily Grind

When Don's family got home from work, ate dinner, and Don finished his homework, only about an
hour remained until it was time for him to get ready
for bed. To free up time, they often ate takeout dinners.
Don was a bit overweight, and the rule was no sweets
in the evening unless he ate his vegetables at dinner.
But other than French fries, he avoided them like the
plague. When he begged for a bedtime snack, they usually gave in. Don was a handful, and they had enough
conflicts as it was. Nor did they want him going to bed
hungry. They figured that if his body was telling him
that he needed a certain snack, they should try to go
along.

Don's parents did not think that spending a lot of
time watching television was good for him. But he was
unhappy at school, and his parents thought he should
have some fun each day. So he watched a couple of
shows in the evenings. Besides, while he was watching
television, his parents could cook, do dishes, tend to the
baby, and perhaps watch a little television themselves.

Don's bedtime was supposed to be at 9:30 on school nights, but he employed all sorts of delaying tactics. In truth, he did not seem to need much sleep, so they did not really push the issue. They were lucky to get him in bed by 11:00.

Modern Dilemmas

Stressed. Exhausted. Overwhelmed. That's how most parents feel much of the time, and if you are the parent of a child with ADD/ADHD, it can be even worse. Eighty percent manage jobs in addition to raising children. Stay-at-home parents struggle to fill in the gap by volunteering at school and handling endless crises for their neighbors. As the rich get richer and more middle-class families slide toward poverty, having two incomes is often the only way to stay a step ahead of the bill collectors. Only a handful of communities have laws requiring companies to pay full-time employees a "living wage" so they can survive on one paycheck. Many single parents have to work overtime or juggle two jobs. Even the lawmakers who declare their support for "family values" have declined to enact legislation so that parents can properly nurture America's future. Governments in Europe provide family leave so that workers can devote time to infant/parent bonding and tend to their youngsters when they are ill or have an emergency. In the United States, the economic cost of such programs is generally considered prohibitive. The emotional cost of not having them takes an indeterminate toll.

 **DID YOU KNOW?**

It really only takes one parent to raise a child. It takes an entire village to support a child's parent. Urge your legislators to pass laws that guarantee workers enough money to support a family on a forty-hour work week. Help your single-parent friends and neighbors.

Make Time for Togetherness

While many parents must paddle frantically to keep from being sucked into a financial sinkhole, many others do not realize that they could in fact work less—and that doing so may be in the ADD/ADHD child's best interest. Most parents are assailed by unending requests for expensive gadgets and garb that their children see advertised on television and that fill the homes of their friends. It is easy for parents to conclude that youngsters' happiness depends more on having material wants gratified than on having parental time and attention. But youngsters benefit more from playing a game of crazy eights with a parent than from playing an expensive video game by themselves. The best possible start in life does not come from the best school money can buy, but from the most loving relationship you can manage. Using your time to play with your child and give him some extra attention may do more to round out children's lives than a schedule packed with lessons and organized activities.

Re-evaluating Priorities

Surveys show the truth of the old saying that money does not buy happiness. Life satisfaction has continued to drop as prosperity has increased. Although growing up in poverty increases family stress, sacrificing time with your children as you quest for more dollars to buy luxuries increases family stress, too, particularly when ADD/ADHD is involved. It may be that you are forced to make some changes.

The Wish for More Family Time

Responses on surveys administered to high school students reveal that the wish for more time with the family is widespread. A minority says that they have as much time with their parents as they would like; the majority say they want to be able to see and talk to their parents more. But time is not the only issue; quality matters, too. On those same surveys, teens also say that they wish that their parents would listen and try to understand them.

Young Materialists

When a youngster voices a wish for more family time, his parents typically defend themselves by saying that they work long hours for their child's benefit. They point out that they would not be able to afford that new bicycle or special pair of shoes their child has been wanting, and he would have to sacrifice trips to restaurants and special activities. When such issues are discussed in family counseling sessions, most children immediately agree to give up the fringe benefits of their parents' paychecks so their parents can work less. They spontaneously start listing ways they could help save money.

What's Best for the Children?

Parents may choose to dedicate long hours to their jobs because the work is fulfilling and they want to enjoy more of life's material pleasures. But they should not assume that working long hours is also best for their children. Youngsters need their parents more than they need trinkets and toys. Many of the songs you sing together in the car will linger in your child's memory for a lifetime. The piles of expensive CDs cluttering the console will soon be forgotten.

The Decline of the Family

Parents used to be their children's heroes, but that has changed. Even members of the tween crowd are more likely to choose a celebrity or popular peer than Mom or Dad for the subject of their "Who I Most Admire" essay. Given how most youngsters spend their time, it is understandable that media stars and peers are esteemed more than parents. Half a century ago, the average U.S. child spent more than three hours a day interacting with parents or extended family members. Today, the average is a mere fifteen minutes. Meanwhile, the average time of watching television each day is four hours. The quality of the time with parents has deteriorated, too, according to parenting author Josh McDowell. He reports that on average, parents spend twelve of their fifteen minutes criticizing, correcting, or teaching their children. That leaves just three minutes a day for conversing and enjoying one another as people.

Make More of an Effort

If your child cares more about what television commercials and peers say about what to buy and wear, it may be important to put more time and energy into strengthening your relationship. If asking about school draws nonanswers (e.g., "Okay," "Fine"), try talking about *your* day. Your youngster cannot feel close to you if he does not know you! Children tend to feel closer to single parents because they share more about what is happening in their lives. This helps to make up for having less time together.

DOES THIS SOUND LIKE YOUR CHILD?

If your child only wants to go on family outings when a friend can come along, watch how you communicate when no guests are present. Be courteous and respectful when dealing with behavior problems. Concentrate on getting to know your child and on having fun.

Quality Time

Many parents struggle to find extracurricular activities that children with ADD/ADHD symptoms can enjoy and use as a steppingstone to making friends. But between daycare, school, and after-school programs, most youngsters have more than enough time with peers. What they really need is more time with their families. That does not mean that they need their parents to spend more time teaching, directing, controlling, and instructing them, however. They need more opportunities to enjoy one another's company. To do that, families need to look for ways to pull themselves out of the daily do-your-homework-and-clean-up-your-room rut that makes everyone tense and edgy.

To free up time, you may need to forego some individual activities if the only real contact is on the trip there and back. Turn off the radio in the car so you can converse while chauffeuring your youngster about town. Being on the soccer field while you chat with other parents in the stands does not count as spending time together. For most families, the biggest time sink is the television.

The Trouble with Television

American teachers have long insisted that watching a lot of television adversely affects students' academic performance and behavior. Educators claim that watching televised stories and movies instead of reading, conversing, and engaging in creative play left students with little imagination. When asked to write a story, many could only relate to an episode from a show they had seen.

TV Causes Restlessness

Children need lots of vigorous exercise, and teachers maintained that sitting in front of the television all evening made students more restless and hyperactive in class. Most veteran teachers expressed the conviction that viewing so much televised sex and violence was contributing to the steady deterioration in behavior and moral values they saw over the years. Others declared that viewing so many commercials was warping children's values. The consensus was that so much stimulation from rapid-fire images had reduced the attention span of the average student to that of a flea. They pointed out that children grew restless at predictable intervals, as if their systems were geared to the rhythm of the once-every-eleven-minutes commercial break. Research investigations examining the impact of television viewing on children's development concluded that the teachers were correct. Children who watch a lot of television are less imaginative and have shorter concentration spans than those who watch none or only an hour per week. Heavy viewers are more easily distracted, more impulsive, more hyperactive, more aggressive, and have more learning problems.

In 2004, research findings on the effects of television made headlines across the country. It was reported that watching a lot of television between birth and age two increased the probability of subsequently being diagnosed with ADD/ADHD by 20 percent! The American Academy of Pediatrics urged parents to protect their babies under age two by not allowing them to watch any television whatsoever. Parents were also advised to limit how much older children watch.

DID YOU KNOW?

Some people believe that families should outlaw television and video games, at least on school nights, to allow time for homework, exercise, and free play. It is harder for children to sit still in school if they sit all evening, too.

TV and Your Child's Development

Physicians conjecture that intense, prolonged visual stimulation of the brain during such a vulnerable stage of life interferes with the development of the central nervous system. If that is true, older children may be adversely affected as well, since their brains are still developing, too. And video games are probably equally dangerous. Be that as it may, it is clear that putting a baby in front of a television program can have serious repercussions. For older children, eliminating television altogether on school days makes good sense. Eliminating it altogether makes even better sense.

Mealtime Amusement

Children clearly need to watch less television, to have wholesome entertainment, to learn how to manage a household, and to consume a well-balanced diet. Youngsters also need more quality time with their parents—and for children, there cannot be quality without a large quantity. Parents need help with housework, to tighten the family budget, and to spend more enjoyable time with their children. The one solution for all of these problems is to stop eating out and turn cooking into a family hobby.

The Kitchen Rules?

To make meal preparation fun, you may need to change the way you operate in the kitchen. When children get involved, their usual role is as the servant. They are told to set the table, pour the beverages, or wash the dishes. Many resent being ordered about and being given the worst jobs. Meanwhile, parents are saddled with all of the responsibility for figuring out what to cook, shopping, doing almost all of the cooking, then battling to get their youngsters to come to the table and eat what they prepared.

A Joint Effort

A happier arrangement for everyone is to turn the job of preparing meals into a partnership. The first step is to include your youngster in the cooking. Even toddlers can shred lettuce for salad, wash radishes, scrub potatoes, butter toast, stir batter, spread peanut butter on celery sticks, and arrange rolls on a plate. Let your child make some of the menu decisions—not just by deciding whether he would prefer spaghetti or pizza, but by pulling out a cookbook and seeing what he would like to learn how to make and serve. Rotate responsibility for the meals. When it is his turn, you will have to help your child, but try to keep him in charge.

- **Let your child create menus.** Going through the cookbook provides practice in reading and learning to think ahead.
- **Let your child create the grocery lists.** It provides great practice for spelling, handwriting, organizing, and learning to think ahead.
- **Let your child shop for the needed groceries.** Checking the ingredients on labels is a great way to practice reading; comparison shopping provides practice using a calculator; learning to stay within a budget is a good way to practice math and decision-making. All of the above are great cures for grocery store misbehavior born of boredom.
- **Let your child be in charge of cooking.** Letting him direct who does what teaches leadership skills. You can keep the chain of command and provide prompts as to what needs to be done by asking, "Do you want me to put the noodles on to boil?"

DID YOU KNOW?

Young chefs are more likely to eat foods they cooked themselves, including the foods they usually disdain. And young farmers who normally gag on vegetables think the ones they have grown themselves are absolutely wonderful. Present your child with seeds and designate a patch of ground for a garden.

To make the time in the kitchen more enjoyable, it is important to talk as well as to listen. Share what is going on in your life and your opinions about happenings in the news. Make it your goal to get to know your child—but remember that for him to open up, he has to know who he is talking to. And if he never does say much about himself, that is fine, too. Many children are doers, not talkers. Spending pleasant time with a parent literally means more to them than words.

Weekend Activities

Finding activities to do together as a family is not hard. Many bicycle stores sponsor Saturday morning family bike rides. Bait and tackle stores hold fishing meets that are open to all ages. Family outings with the Sierra Club for hikes and with other nature groups for birdwatching expeditions are fun and provide great exercise. Mountain Man clubs are for women, too, and participants whittle, cook meals over open fires, tan leather, and engage in lots of other old-time activities that fascinate children.

Get Involved!

Help connect your youngster to the community by donating time to neighborhood cleanups or another worthy cause, such as Habitat for Humanity and local homeless shelters. Seeing the realities of poverty up close does more to convince children about the need for education and a career than a thousand lectures. Make it a habit to read the weekend guide of your local paper, and set a goal to attend at least one activity each month until you find a hobby or activity the whole family can enjoy. After a trip to a garden show, you may decide to get serious about growing tulips. A visit to a cat show may convince you that raising fabulous felines or volunteering at the local animal shelter is a project that everyone can get behind. Some families spend years building a boat in the garage. The boat may never see water, but the shared dreams and the hours spent tinkering bring parents and children closer.

DID YOU KNOW?

Churches, synagogues, mosques, and temples offer a wealth of family activities. If you are not religious, try attending a different one each week. That way your child can experience them all while learning about the many fascinating customs. Afterward, you will have lots of fodder for interesting conversations.

Adapt Your Lifestyle

After realizing the impact of their family's lifestyle on Don's ADD/ADHD symptoms, his parents decided to make some dramatic changes. They were all cranky the first week after they got rid of the television, because they did not know another way to relax. Don considered the loss of the television a form of child abuse. They started cooking dinner together and taking walks afterward. It was cold and rainy, so they bundled up and carried umbrellas. Don's parents belted out renditions of "Singin' in the Rain," while Don glowered and acted as though he might die of embarrassment. In addition to a bedtime story, they started reading a book aloud that they could all enjoy. Don sat on the floor and played with Legos, yawning noisily at regular intervals to indicate his disdain for the story.

Losing Control

Don's parents were determined to keep the project of cooking dinner together relaxed and enjoyable. However, his mother began to cave in under their son's unrelenting ill humor. As she was at the sink spraying the lettuce one evening, Don started carrying on that she could fix him a salad but could not make him eat it. She just lost it. She grabbed a handful of lettuce and hurled it onto the floor in anger. "OK! There's your salad! You do not have to eat it!" she snapped. Everyone froze in horror, and she was appalled at what she had done. "I guess I need to cool it, huh?" she asked meekly, turning the sprayer on herself. "What in the world . . . ?" her husband demanded. "You need to cool it, too," she said, turning the sprayer on him.

DID YOU KNOW?

A family outing to a farmer's market is an important educational experience for city kids, and visiting can improve your child's attitude toward vegetables. Let her make some of the selections and handle all of the financial transactions.

One thing led to another, and they ended up in a riotous food fight that took days to clean up and that still made Don chuckle when he told the story to his own children decades later. It was an unorthodox way to get the family onto a happier footing. But the magic of shared laughter turned Don around. Not only did Don start eating salads, but the next time his parents belted out "Singin' in the Rain" as they walked down the block, he joined in.

Chapter 7

Anger, Organization, and Worry—Emotional Struggles

10 Things You Will Learn in This Chapter

- How to recognize and avoid emotional triggers
- Many defiant children are in pain and in need of your support
- The many different ways in which angry feelings can be expressed
- How nagging and criticizing are unproductive and rarely bring about change
- How you could be mistaking your son's sadness and fear for anger
- The three indications that your child is ready to understand your punishment and learn from it
- How to help toddlers talk about their feelings so they learn to recognize them themselves
- Tactics that will soothe your child during a tantrum and move him past it
- Help your child organize in his/her own way—which will have a more lasting effect!

Understanding Your Angry Child

Some children are so hypersensitive, anything and everything sets them off. Other chronically angry youngsters are reacting to how they are treated. Many parents who see themselves as strict disciplinarians come across as harsh and rejecting. The modern style is to be over-indulgent and to tolerate a good deal of misbehavior, then frazzled parents explode when they reach the end of their rope. Other youngsters are irritable because they do not feel well physically. They do not realize that anything is wrong because they always feel about the same. They suffer from chronic sleep deprivation, lack of exercise, stress, lead poisoning, toxic overload from pollutants, food allergies, and/or poor nutrition.

Figuring Out Why

Food allergies are a more widespread cause of crankiness and irritability than most parents realize. Several studies on prison inmates found that previously undiagnosed nutritional allergies are rampant among this chronically angry, very aggressive, and sometimes violent population. The increase in food allergies in the general population has been astronomical. Peanut allergies alone doubled between 1997 and 2002 to affect 600,000 children, and even parents who try to protect their allergic child's diet usually find they cannot. Food manufacturers have thwarted labeling laws by listing the names of common allergens in Latin or as "natural flavoring." In 2006, the FDA actually changed food labels in order to make it easier for people to recognize the ingredients that may cause these food allergies.

DID YOU KNOW?

One researcher suggested that chronic sleep deprivation may explain why children taking stimulants do not improve academically despite their better classroom behavior and attentiveness. Stimulant medication settles them down but produces insomnia. They can concentrate better but remain unable to think clearly.

Understanding Anger

Sometimes anger is a mask for fear, as when an abused child's fight-or-flight response is stuck on "fight" from having been repeatedly terrorized. Some children seem to be addicted to anger and appear to search for things to be mad about. Still others have learned that their anger gets results, so they keep using it. But for most children most of the time, anger is an important, useful, and normal emotion, even if it is unpleasant for their parents. Anger is not necessarily destructive, as some parents and professionals maintain. People who grew up in violent households often equate anger with rage, but these two emotions are not the same. The goal of anger management is not to make your youngster's anger disappear, but to teach him to use it so that it works for him rather than against him.

Anger 101

The emotion of anger varies in intensity from mild disapproval to blind rage. In between those extremes are dissatisfaction, displeasure, crankiness, irritation, resentment, aggravation, frustration, indignation, exasperation, enmity, animosity, ire, hate, wrath, and fury. Angry feelings are the internal signals that let people know that some sort of change is needed. Accordingly, they have important survival value. By screaming to get their parents' attention, hungry infants are more likely to be fed than if they passively wait for someone to offer up some sustenance. During the days of the cave dwellers, mobilizing aggression to fend off marauding tribes and animals increased the chances that a clan could hold onto its family members and food supply. Lots of angry children would have made great warriors!

DOES THIS SOUND LIKE YOUR CHILD?

Beneath the tough exteriors of many defiant children are youngsters in pain. Criticism causes them to retreat further into their shells. Focusing on what they do right can help build trust that you are on their side. Start commenting on small accomplishments!

Anger provides the impetus for children and adults alike to protect themselves, to confront obstacles, to right wrongs, and to make the world a better place for themselves and others. Whether angry feelings are triggered by real or imaginary events is actually irrelevant; the feelings are the same in either case. In many ways, anger is like pain. It may be very unpleasant, but it is not in and of itself good or bad, right or wrong. It is the signal that lets people know that something is wrong. It makes as little sense to say, "You have no right to be angry" as it makes to say, "You have no right to be in pain." How people express their feelings is another matter altogether.

Anger in Action

Angry feelings can be expressed through body language (from rolling the eyes to raising a fist), verbally (from whining to making threats), and through action (from pulling a classmate's pony-tail to committing murder and mayhem). It is possible to feel angry and not express it. Some children express anger in such convoluted ways that their parents do not know that anger is an issue. An example is the child who cries over homework, not because he is sad or worried, but because he is angry that his parents are making him do it.

A BETTER PARENTING PRACTICE

If your child purposely destroys a toy, ask what he is angry about. He may not answer, because he may not know. But the question will prompt him to consider the matter. When he can identify and say what he is angry about, you may be able to help him find solutions to whatever is upsetting him.

Constant pleas for help can then ensure that if he must suffer, his parents must suffer along with him. Some children internalize their angry feelings and turn them back onto themselves or their possessions. They destroy their toys or harangue themselves for being worthless. Often the torrent of self-directed rage is triggered by something that someone else said or did that angered them. Being angry at oneself can feel safer than being angry with someone else.

A BETTER PARENTING PRACTICE

Nagging and criticizing are parental expressions of anger that rarely bring about change. Pick a problem, discuss it with your child when you are both calm, define some clear rules, and work out straightforward consequences.

Keeping too much anger inside can be dangerous. It is like turning up the heat on a pressure cooker and failing to open the vent to let the steam out—sooner or later, there is an explosion. Many children keep a tight lid on their anger at school during the day and explode at siblings when they get home. Others contain their anger at home and release it at school. Some children keep their anger inside for years and it seems to eat away at them. Digestive ailments and other psychosomatic disorders were once thought to result from keeping anger inside, though it turns out that stress in general rather than anger in particular may be responsible. School shootings and teen suicides are tragic examples of the consequences of storing too much anger.

Teaching Anger Management
Psychologists used to believe that airing grievances via no-holds-barred verbal confrontations was a good way to clear the air. They now know that such an approach is destructive. It undermined relationships, worsened

hostilities, and caused people to say vicious things they did not mean and could not later take back. Therapists began providing assertiveness training to teach family members how to broach disagreements in a considerate, respectful, and controlled manner.

DID YOU KNOW?

Besides being more aggressive than girls, boys act out more because it is harder for them to identify and express their feelings with words. Before admonishing your son not to cry or be scared, consider the alternative! Too many boys express sadness and fear as anger.

You may feel that your child explodes and has tantrums out of the blue, is resentful or destructive for no reason, and is vindictive and spiteful without cause. Before you can help your youngster manage anger appropriately, you must accept that there is in fact a reason for his anger. Detecting the reason can be difficult. Because infants can only howl when they want something, they end up doing a lot of angry crying. They do not actually know what they want—they only know that they are uncomfortable. Their parents must try to figure out what is wrong. They may be hungry and need to be fed, lonely and need to be held, wet and need a diaper change, or have a tummyache and need to be burped. After having their needs met time and again, infants begin to associate certain physical discomforts with what helps them to feel better.

Steps for Handling Anger

To manage anger appropriately, children must be able to do three things:

1. Identify their wants and desires
2. Communicate their wants and desires
3. Cope when their wishes are not gratified

Many parents overlook the first two steps and skip to the third. That means they are trying to get their youngster to settle down and contain himself when they do not even know what is wrong. Many do not even consider that their child needs or wants something, and automatically conclude that he is angry for no reason. If a four-year-old is screaming for another cookie when he has not yet eaten the one he is holding in his hand, the reason may be that he is sleep-deprived, stressed, or actually upset about something else altogether. But trust that there is a reason!

Identifying Feelings

By the time they are toddlers, children should have learned to identify many of their needs and wants. They can often point or use words to signal their desire to be fed, changed, played with, or handed a toy, and parents spend less time having to guess what is upsetting them. Some children are more adept at identifying feelings than others. Girls usually find it easier than boys. Still, learning is a lifelong task. Parents need to help by saying, "You look tired," "You sound happy," "You must be thirsty," "You seem excited." Reading body language is an inexact science at best; only your child can know for sure what she is feeling. The point of commenting is to get your child to consider her feelings so she can learn to identify them. Be sure to ask what is wrong whenever your youngster is upset. Your youngster may not know the answer, but asking will encourage her to engage in a bit of introspection so she can eventually become better at deciphering her feelings.

Communicating Feelings

To teach a toddler who is about to deck another child how to express anger appropriately, take the flying fists in your hands and teach him how to put his feelings into words, saying, "You must not hit her! Tell her you want your toy back. Can you say 'my toy'?" Many older children do not put their angry feelings into words, and they benefit from the same sort of lessons by being given the proper words to use.

When children do not believe that they have been heard or properly understood, they repeat themselves, whine, raise their voices, and become increasingly frustrated. Make it a habit to summarize what you think your child is attempting to communicate whenever she is upset. "You are mad about having to carry a lunch to school because you want to buy it in the cafeteria." "You are upset because you want to go out and play and do your homework later."

Do You Know What the Problem Is?

It is easy for parents to assume they know what the problem is; too often they jump to the wrong conclusion.

And just knowing that their parent understands often keeps children from having to create a major scene to get their point across. For children with certain personality types, being heard and understood is often enough to soothe them. When they are upset over a run-in with a teacher, friend, or sibling, they do not need someone to fix their problem. They merely need to be understood, although they may also appreciate compassion. A simple hug or statement such as, "I'm sorry that happened to you" is enough to restore their good humor.

Learning to Tolerate Frustration

Often youngsters need more than a sympathetic ear; they need some concrete help to solve whatever problem is making them angry. After they identify and communicate what is upsetting them, the next step is to teach them to cope when they cannot have what they want when they want it. Learning to delay gratification and tolerate frustration tends to improve as children mature, so they recover from disappointments with less upset. But not every youngster figures out how to do that without help. When your child is angry, respond by offering comfort, perhaps by saying, "I know you are disappointed about not being able to have candy. If you are hungry, I'll fix you something when we get home." Depending on your tone of voice, you can communicate empathy, compassion, and a willingness to meet your child's needs. After hearing many similar comments, your youngster will learn to talk himself through similar situations. Then instead of grabbing for the candy bar when he is in college, he may be able to wait to eat until he gets back to his apartment and can fix himself a decent meal.

DID YOU KNOW?

Many children with ADD/ADHD are especially sensitive to thirst, hunger, temperature changes, pain, etc. Have water, a snack, a sweater, comfortable shoes, etc., in the car. She needs to learn to anticipate her needs.

Change the Subject

Responding to continuing howls by starting a conversation on another subject can be a way to communicate what people must do when they are angry about something they cannot change: they need to move on. Thinking about other things can help. Howling can be a way for children to discharge some of their anger, which helps them to calm down. When they finally do, it is understandable that a parent is reluctant to say, "I'm glad you're feeling better" for fear the youngster will remember his previous distress and start howling again. But at some point it is essential to point out, "You were really upset when you could not have the candy you wanted, but you calmed down." Children need to know they can cope and recover—that their feelings change and their anger passes. When they can count on being heard and comforted or learn to turn their thoughts to something else, they acquire the ability to soothe and distract themselves. That will not stop them from getting angry, but it will ensure they have some essential skills for coping with life's frustrations and disappointments.

If your child seems to have an excessive amount of anger or just can't ever seem to get it under control, he may have a coexisting disorder such as depression or bipolar disorder. Make sure you remember to bring this up with your child's treating professional.

Organizational Learning

Most parents have an intuitive understanding of why organizational skills are important. They have lots of experience organizing everything from meals and linen closets to car pools and birthday parties. In order to teach their child to organize, they also need to grasp the concrete benefits so they can explain them and boost their youngster's motivation to learn. They need to know the precise steps involved so they can walk their youngster through the steps.

A New Beginning

To set the stage for a new beginning, tell your child that perhaps cleaning up his bedroom and keeping track of his school papers and possessions have been hard because you did not sit down and teach him how to organize them. An apology for not having provided enough help can be a good way to extend an olive branch and convince a defiant youngster that you are on his side. Explain the benefits of learning to organize a bedroom and notebook and keep them in order: It will be easier for him to find his things. He can use the same skills to organize his school desk, locker, backpack, toys, collections, and computer files. There will be fewer frustrations and upsets over misplaced and lost possessions.

Organizing 101

Organizing objects of any kind entails putting related items into a group and storing them together in a specific location, such as clothes in a closet, toys in a cabinet, school supplies in a drawer, soiled clothes in a laundry hamper, school papers in a notebook, etc. It is obvious to parents that it is easier to find a particular worksheet if papers are kept in a notebook than if they are randomly tucked into various pockets, books, and folders, and it is easier to find a pair of clean socks if all of them are kept in the same drawer. This is not necessarily obvious to children, however. Parents need to explain that although organizing takes some time and effort up front, it saves lots of time and many headaches in the long run.

DID YOU KNOW?

Someday your child will need to keep an entire house and an office, desk, or work area in order. The best way to prepare is by teaching him how to manage his bedroom and school papers—and helping him develop the discipline to actually keep them organized.

With a good organizational system, your child should be able to locate any item in about two seconds. If much more time is needed, that usually means the group is too large. In that case, the usual procedure is to divide the group by creating some new categories. For instance, most students put their school papers into different sections of a notebook or keep them in separate folders so they can find individual papers more easily. Different students use different systems, but the usual approach is to group papers by subject. If it is still hard to locate a particular item, some of the sections may need to be subdivided. The papers for social studies, arithmetic, spelling, etc., could be divided so that homework assignments, tests, and notes are stored separately. There are several simple steps for organizing objects:

1. Putting related items into a group
2. Deciding where to store them
3. Dividing large groups into sections and/or ordering the items

These steps apply to any task that involves organizing objects. A child might organize her video collection by putting the comedies and dramas in different areas of the cabinet. If it is still hard to find one that she wants to see, she could create a separate category for cartoons or could alphabetize them by title.

A BETTER PARENTING PRACTICE

Many parents decide where their youngster should store her toys, books, and clothing. However, the arrangement that seems sensible to them may not be convenient or make sense to their child. That makes it hard for her to find things and to know where to put them when tidying up.

Bedroom Management

Accompany your child to the bedroom and tell him that you will help him figure out how to organize all of his things in a way that works for him. Explain that a group of related objects can be organized in many different ways. Books can be lined up on a shelf by height, color, subject, or alphabetically by title or author. They can be arranged so that reference books are grouped together on one side of the bookcase and the rest of the books are in no particular order. People usually put things they rarely use in the back of a closet, in the middle of a notebook, or on a high shelf and store frequently used items in more accessible locations. However, special collections and objects with sentimental value are often placed within easy reach on desks and dresser tops even though they are rarely used.

What's the Point?

The point of organizing is to make it easier for your child to find and put away his things, so he really needs to be in charge of the decisions about where his possessions are kept. Determining the arrangement also deepens children's sense of connection to their personal space, which can heighten their desire to keep it clean and in order. It is fine to explain why *you* keep your jeans and pajamas in separate drawers, but try to honor your child's wishes even if you do not agree with them. As you go through his things together, ask where he would like to keep everything from his socks to his toys. Help him sort and arrange, but have him make the decisions. If he chooses unusual places to put things, so be it. Just be sure to repeat the key question often: When he wants to find or put away his baseball mitt, will he be able to remember that it is with the school supplies that he has chosen to store in a box under his bed?

Coming up with the perfect bedroom arrangement the first time through is not necessarily desirable; your child will learn more by experimenting to see what works best. Offer to help him rearrange his things if he wants to try a different organizational system in the future.

Organizing School Papers

Organizing school papers simply involves designating different sections of a notebook or different folders for particular subjects. Each section or folder should be organized so that homework, projects, class notes, quizzes, and tests are in some sort of logical order. One possibility is to organize the papers by date, with the most recent papers on top so they are readily accessible.

A student may feel overwhelmed if it is late in the semester, her papers are in total disarray, and her notebook needs a complete overhaul. By sitting at her side to help her figure out where to put each paper, you can start teaching her how to organize, provide some solid hands-on practice, and help her straighten out her notebook all at the same time. Whether the job is finished in a single sitting or after several sessions, the secret is to communicate the goal clearly: to create a system so that any paper can be located and filed quickly. Sit down every school evening and help her file the miscellaneous papers until she can handle her papers by herself. At the start of each school year, help her organize a new notebook.

A BETTER PARENTING PRACTICE

Your teenager may insist that her messy room is her own affair. But being able to care for a bedroom is an important skill. It prepares teens to take care of a home. Your child will benefit from the time you spend teaching and monitoring.

Projects: Task by Task

Projects that seem simple to an adult can seem overwhelming to a child. Many youngsters are accused of procrastinating when the real problem is that they are frozen due to confusion or fear. They feel lost because they do not know how to get started. Or they do not think they can finish because of a problem they expect to encounter or have already run up against. Since children are often unable to identify or describe the problem, their parents and teachers may assume their lack of progress is due to laziness.

Method Instead of Madness

The method for organizing projects such as getting ready for school in the morning and doing a book report is the same as for organizing a neighborhood club, wedding, or a multinational company. It is important for youngsters to understand that once they learn to organize small projects, they will be able to organize big ones with equal ease. Organizing a project involves dividing it into a series of simple, straightforward tasks:

1. List the tasks.
2. List the materials and special resources needed for each task.
3. Put the tasks in order.
4. Review the list of tasks and mark those that seem difficult.
5. Divide difficult tasks into a series of steps.
6. Review the list of steps and mark those that seem difficult.
7. Divide difficult steps into a series of smaller steps.
8. Review the list of smaller steps and mark those that seem difficult.
9. Brainstorm ways to get help with difficult steps.

After each task is finished, it should be checked off. The trick is to make sure that the child considers each task on the list to be simple and straightforward. If one of the tasks seems too hard, the solution is usually to subdivide it into a series of small steps. If one of the steps seems too difficult, it should be subdivided into a series of still smaller steps. If a step cannot be made any smaller and it still seems too hard, that usually signals a need for outside help. But after having subdivided the steps several times, the child should be able to identify the sticking point and be able to identify exactly what kind of help he needs.

Define "Complicated"

For many children diagnosed with ADD/ADHD, having to do a lot of homework can seem like a huge, complicated project. Some avoid it like the plague; others run to parents and teachers every two minutes with desperate appeals for help. When parents try to find out what the problem is, their youngster may only be able to say, "I don't know what to do." If children start by listing the tasks they need to do for each subject, chances are that the project will look pretty straightforward to them. However, it may turn out that some of the assignments seem hard. The solution is to list all of the steps involved, review them, and subdivide any that still look difficult. You will probably need to provide lots of help breaking tasks into steps and ministeps until your child learns how.

A BETTER PARENTING PRACTICE

Sit down with your child each evening and show him how to record assignments, tasks, and steps in a homework planner until he can handle the job himself. Help him divide up long projects that span several evenings and enter the steps into the planner on the appropriate dates.

Subdivide and Conquer

If an assignment to do twenty math problems seems overly intimidating, they might be subdivided into two steps consisting of ten problems each. If that still seems too hard, they could be subdivided into four sets of five problems or ten sets of two. If the first step that consists of two problems still seems hard, it might be subdivided into steps that include reviewing the appropriate section of the textbook, reading the directions, working the examples, contacting a classmate for help, and doing two problems. Project plans can be long, which can make them seem even more overwhelming than a brief note to "do the problems on page 64." Urge your child to concentrate on one step at a time and not to worry about the rest.

Tuesday's Homework

Task 1: Math Homework

    Step 1   Do problems 1 and 2

        Ministep 1   Review the textbook

        Ministep 2   Read the directions

        Ministep 3   Work the examples

        Ministep 4   Do problems 1 and 2

        Ministep 5   Have Dad check to see that I'm doing them right

    Step 2   Do problems 3–10

    Step 3   Problems 10–20

    Step 4   Have Dad check my work

Task 2: Spelling
>   **Step 1**   Homework—do the worksheet
>   **Step 2**   Study for test on Friday
>   Ministep 1   Learn to spell 4 words

Teaching Time Management

Prioritizing is a basic time-management skill. A good time to help your child learn is when helping him decide on the order for doing homework assignments. Some students prefer to do the easiest ones first, because it boosts their confidence. Others prefer to tackle the harder items first because they are fresher, and they can relax once those are finished. Help your child list the tasks and put them in order before he sets out to do any project that has given him difficulty in the past. Consider making and posting lists in convenient locations to guide him through washing the dishes, straightening his room, and packing his bookbag. Children with poor memories for such details should use as many aids as possible. After referring to their lists and checking off each completed task and step over a period of weeks, months, or years, they will undoubtedly memorize the procedure.

The Passage of Time

Children diagnosed with ADD/ADHD tend to be remarkably unaware of the passage of time. As a consequence, they commonly misjudge how much time is required to complete routine tasks. A common pattern is to underestimate how long it will take them to get ready to go somewhere or do a chore, and to exaggerate the amount of time they spend on activities they dislike. Poor students commonly report that they do an hour of homework every evening, when they actually average only about fifteen or twenty minutes.

DID YOU KNOW?

Knowing how much time is actually required to complete chores can make them easier to face, and working on them for shorter periods of time at a stretch sometimes makes them a lot less arduous.

How Long Will This Take?

To learn to cope with deadlines, youngsters need to be able to judge how much time various projects will take and set up schedules matched to their capabilities and, whenever possible, their desires. The first step is to collect lots of data about how long it takes them to do all kinds of routine tasks: taking a bath, completing a set of math problems, gathering their things together for baseball practice, walking home from a friend's house, etc. That information will eventually enable them to make realistic estimates about how much time they need to allow themselves for various tasks. Fortunately, most children get a kick out of timing themselves and enjoy searching for ways to do disliked projects more efficiently so they can finish them faster. Becoming a time management expert can be a lot of fun.

Getting Ready on Time

To get ready for school on time in the morning, children can follow the same procedures as they do for managing other projects. They list all of the tasks, and then review the list to pinpoint difficult ones. They divide the hard tasks into a series of simpler steps and identify the areas where they need help. They put all of the tasks in order and note the special materials and help they need for each step. They then need to create a schedule. The first step is to determine how much time they need for each task so that they can get ready on time. Most children enjoy timing themselves to see how long it takes them to get out of bed after they are called, get dressed, eat breakfast, wash their hands, brush their teeth, collect their belongings, etc. That information can be used to figure out when to get up in the morning so they can move at a comfortable pace and be ready to leave the house on time. After working out a schedule, many youngsters enjoy setting an alarm on a watch to notify them when it is time to proceed to the next activity.

A BETTER PARENTING PRACTICE

Your child may need to eat breakfast at a particular time, but let her control her morning schedule as much as possible. Lingering in bed for a few minutes after being awakened and being able to dawdle after breakfast may get her day off to a happier start.

Plan as Much as Possible

To free up time in the morning, many children decide to do some of their morning chores the night before. They decide what to wear, lay out clothes, make lunch, and pack their bookbag. When a child is allowed to work out his own schedule, his parents are often amazed to hear him decide on an earlier bedtime so he can get up earlier and not be so rushed in the morning. Nagging during a madcap race to get out the door day after day is as miserable for children as for their parents. Once youngsters have the time management skills to avoid such unpleasantness, most are happy to use them.

Does Your Child Internalize Behaviors and Anxiety?

When adults are anxious, they typically become agitated, cannot sit still, and are so restless that they may pace. They have trouble sleeping and are cranky, irritable, and distracted. They have difficulty concentrating, make poor decisions, and act impulsively. Anxious children are the same, except that instead of pacing, they engage in a lot of disorganized activity. What they need most is to learn to relax. A number of treatments are available to help them learn to control their thoughts and calm down.

Longing for Answers

Parents of children with ADD/ADHD symptoms commonly engage in a lengthy quest for the correct diagnosis, believing that when it is found, the correct treatment can be started. They become increasingly confused and overwhelmed when every doctor they consult comes up with a different diagnosis. Many conclude that "head doctors" are incompetent and have nothing to offer. In truth, psychology remains in its infancy. The day may come when knowing the exact diagnosis will dictate the precise form of treatment, but psychology remains more art than science. It is more helpful for parents to direct their attention to two main types of difficulties: internalizing and externalizing behaviors.

Externalizers

Children who act out their feelings are said to be engaging in externalizing behaviors. They are aggressive, oppositional, and defiant. Externalizers are overwhelmingly male. Because they are so disruptive, many are diagnosed with ADHD. Children who "act in" or internalize their distress often experience anxiety, exaggerated fears, and depression. They are often diagnosed with ADD. On the outside, they show signs of nervous tension by biting their nails, twirling or pulling their hair, engaging in rituals, or through psychosomatic illnesses. On the inside, their racing minds are filled with worries, commonly about grades and tests, a parent dying or being injured, or burglars invading their house at night.

Internalizers

The percentages of children with externalizing and internalizing behaviors are estimated to be about the same. But because internalizers are usually anxious to please adults and to follow rules, they tend not to be as disruptive. That can make them easy to overlook, and such youngsters are less likely to receive special psychological or educational assistance than those who act out. Some children engage in both externalizing and internalizing behaviors. They are aggressive and defiant, and also have significant problems with anxiety, fear, and depression. They are often diagnosed with the combined type of ADD/ADHD. This difficult mix is common among children with attachment problems. Attachment therapy, an experimental but controversial treatment, may help them. See *www.instituteforattachment.org*.

Internalizing behaviors tend to be fairly stable throughout childhood. Overly anxious, fearful seven-year-olds are likely to have similar emotional difficulties at age fourteen, with depression often intensifying during adolescence. Since children do not usually outgrow their tendency to be fearful, nervous, and depressed, it is important to teach them how to control their thoughts and manage their emotions.

Reassure Your Worrywart, Talk Through Trouble
Talking can be a good way for children to relieve worries, and you may be able to find simple solutions to problems that have kept your youngster tossing and turning at night and biting her fingernails during the day. Some little perfectionists are convinced that having lost a library book is the ultimate crime, and that they will never be forgiven. Reassurance that accidents happen may not be enough to put their minds at ease. Offer to help look for the book and explain that if it

cannot be found, paying the replacement fee will satisfy the librarian. To err is human; knowing how to correct errors afterward is divine. For many youngsters, the big challenge is teaching them to reach out for help when they have a problem.

A Deeper Issue?

Sometimes the things children worry about reflect deeper issues, and identifying them requires some detective work. Starting a new school year sends many youngsters into a tizzy. They worry that the work will be too hard, the teacher too mean, or they will not be able to find their classroom. Reassurance does not get very far, because the real issue is their fear of the unknown. Scheduling an appointment to meet the teacher before the school starts can do a lot to restore their calm.

DOES THIS SOUND LIKE YOUR CHILD?

When people are anxious, the muscles in the chest tighten, which prevents them from getting enough oxygen. Encourage your youngster to take some deep breaths when he is upset and to concentrate on the rise and fall of his abdomen to block worrisome thoughts.

Similarly, turning on the light in a youngster's bedroom to prove that no monsters are hiding in the closet or under the bed rarely helps for more than a moment or two. As soon as the light is turned off and the parent departs, the child's uneasiness about being alone in a darkened room returns. What these youngsters need is to have their underlying feelings of helplessness and vulnerability addressed. Providing a magic flashlight to stave off monsters may be enough to restore their sense of being powerful and in control. Similarly, rubbing a magic stone or amulet to activate its protective powers whenever a child senses that a parent might be in danger can relieve separation anxiety.

Happy Thoughts

Learning to stop thinking about problems that cannot be solved at the moment is an important skill. Help your child learn to distract himself by telling him to think happy thoughts, and help him do it by telling a funny story or having a tickle session. Save his favorite jokes, cartoons, and funny e-mails to reread when he needs to lighten up. Meditating for ten minutes is an effective quick fix for stress and worry, and daily practice can bring about lasting changes.

Confronting Worries Head-On

If your little worrywart cannot stop thinking that lightning might strike the house, terrorists are going to attack the country, or some natural or manmade disaster is going to lead to your demise, provide some simple reassurance. Let your child know that the disasters she fears will not come to pass, or that if something bad does happen it will be dealt with. If that is not enough, it may help to play out a terrible possibility your child is fixated on to its grisly conclusion.

Spell It Out

If lightning were to strike and the house burned down, what then? All of the family pictures and mementos would be lost. The family would have to find a new house, but at least you would all be together. If terrorists attacked the country, lots of people might be killed. There would be lots of heartache and suffering. But the army would protect the survivors and life would go on. If you were to die in a car crash, keel over with a heart attack, or be whisked away by kidnappers, acknowledge that your child would of course be terribly sad. Tell her who would finish raising her. Let her know that you would want her to treasure the happy memories and go on to have a happy life. Then, try to lighten her mood with a little humor—perhaps by telling her that you want your ashes placed in a gift box covered with Snoopy wrapping paper and placed on her desk. That way you can keep tabs on what she is up to, and if she does not make her bed in the morning or leaves her clothes on the floor, you will haunt her from the Great Beyond.

Relaxation, Meditation, and Control

People cannot be physically relaxed and emotionally upset at the same time, so an effective way to relax the mind is to relax the body. Psychologists have developed some relaxation exercises for that purpose. Do the exercises yourself while guiding your youngster through the steps to get a better feel for how they work and to avoid moving too fast or too slow. Have your child sit in a comfortable chair. Speak slowly in a soothing voice.

Children tend to be nervous the first time through, and some respond by acting silly. It is usually better to ignore disruptions and continue. Getting angry will not help your child relax! Youngsters are usually more cooperative after they have been through the entire exercise once and understand how it goes.

Relaxing on Cue

Deep muscle relaxation involves tensing and then relaxing the major muscle groups to heighten awareness of the physical sensations. With practice, children can learn to relax on cue. Have your child close his eyes and take some long, deep breaths, inhaling as you count to five and then exhaling slowly. Next, tell him that when you say "go," he is to tense the muscles in his legs, making them as tight as he possibly can. He should curl his toes, stiffen his ankles, feel his calves go into a knot, and tense his thighs until his feet come off the floor and his legs begin to tremble. Count to five, telling him to try to make the muscles even tighter as you count. Then tell him to relax all at once and to notice the sensations of heaviness and warmth as the tension is released from his muscles.

DID YOU KNOW?

After doing deep muscle relaxation for ten minutes a day for a few weeks, your child should be able to relax all of his muscles instantly. Tell him to use this technique to calm himself whenever he is feeling tense, worried, angry, or "hyper."

After having tensed and relaxed his legs, tell your child to raise his arms to shoulder level. He should tense all of the muscles by making fists, locking his elbows, and tightening his lower and upper arms. He should continue to tighten his muscles as you count to five, until his arms are trembling from the exertion. Then tell him to relax the muscles and let his arms drop to his sides. After spending a moment noticing the sensations of warmth and relaxation in his arms and hands, instruct him to tighten his abdomen and buttocks. Tightening these muscles is similar to straining to have a bowel movement. After counting to five, tell him to let all of those muscles relax, then concentrate on how they feel. Proceed by having him tense his upper chest, shoulders, and face. He should raise his shoulders as high as he can, clench his teeth, draw back his lips toward his ears, and squeeze his eyes shut. Once again, have him release all of the muscles and notice the sensations of relaxation. Finally, he tenses all of the muscles in his body at the same time, keeps them tight for five seconds, and releases and sinks into the chair. Tell him to sit for a moment and notice how it feels to be completely relaxed.

Meditation

Parents constantly tell hyperactive children to settle down, but that does not teach them how! The popular practice of sending rowdy children to timeout misses the point. Timeouts help by removing them from situations that are overly stimulating. They drive home the message that rowdy behavior is unacceptable and provide parents with respite. But there is no guarantee that a child will discover the key to calming down while sitting in timeout. One solution is to teach your child to meditate. Then have him sit down and practice in lieu of assigning a traditional timeout.

Meditating may lessen or solve other behavioral problems as well. EEGs and various brain imaging techniques have found some notable differences between the brain waves and blood flow, especially in the frontal lobes, of children diagnosed with ADD/ADHD. Transcendental meditation is a proven method for normalizing both, and this type of meditation can be readily taught to children. Research shows that meditating regularly produces a host of benefits, including improved impulse control, increased IQ, and enhanced cognitive functioning.

A BETTER PARENTING PRACTICE

Some people spend a lifetime studying meditation. They sit in the lotus position and practice for hours on end. However, parents can teach by providing a brief explanation, walking their child through the steps, and practicing together at home for brief periods each day.

Meditation classes abound. They are offered through continuing education programs at local colleges, parks and recreation departments, yoga centers, Buddhist temples, and through private instructors. Parents can sign up for a class and then teach their youngster at home. Or they can read about the techniques and purchase instructional materials online. Meditating just ten minutes a day can yield substantial benefits. It is a much more effective way to relax than watching television! Put on Jim Malloy's CD, *The Complete Meditation Class,* available at *www.meditationcenter.com*, and let his soothing voice guide you.

Many Different Approaches

There are many approaches to meditation. One is to sit still in a comfortable chair in a quiet room, eyes closed, and tell your child to concentrate on breathing, so that his only awareness is the sensation of air entering and leaving his body. Tell him to imagine that he is inhaling peaceful feelings of tranquility and relaxation with each breath he takes, and that he is releasing worries, negative thoughts, and tension each time he exhales. It is a myth that people should try to turn off their thoughts or make their mind go blank. The mere act of trying increases tension. Suggest that when his mind wanders, he gently return his focus of attention to his breath.

DID YOU KNOW?

After learning to meditate, children can calm down by concentrating on their breathing for a moment whenever they feel scattered, restless, or "hyper." But emergency fixes may not be needed very often if they practice meditating ten minutes a day. They will probably be calmer, more alert, and more focused.

Different people prefer different ways of meditating. Instead of concentrating on breathing, some children find it more helpful to close their eyes and concentrate on the patterns of light behind their eyelids. The goal should not be to analyze or interpret them, but just to be aware of them. Others find it works better to keep their eyes open but unfocused as they relax their eyelids and gaze downward. If their mind wanders or they find themselves staring at an object, they should let their eyes go out of focus again and return their attention to their unfocused gaze.

It's Not So Easy!

The mere act of sitting still to meditate is not easy for anyone at first, and it is especially hard for hyperactive children. Restlessness and urges to shift about can be intense. Although youngsters should be encouraged to remain still, they obviously cannot relax while fighting the urge to move. If they need to wriggle or persist in swinging their leg, it is better for them to do it. Many children react to the novelty of the situation with silliness. It is usually better to ignore misbehavior. Continue to speak slowly in a soothing tone as you tell your youngster to note the sensation of air entering and leaving his nostrils, of his diaphragm opening and closing, of his chest rising and falling. Instruct him to imagine feelings of relaxation being inhaled with each breath and moving down to his toes and out into his fingers.

Chapter 8

Dealing with Difficult Behavior

10 Things You Will Learn in This Chapter

- How a behavior modification program can save your sanity

- How to ask "nicely" and achieve understanding

- Why setting small obtainable goals and offering rewards will affect long-term success

- Why you should develop a list of behaviors you want to eliminate or to increase

- How the main reason behavior modification fails is because of the parent, not the child!

- Why you have to watch the balance between material and social rewards

- Why your child's involvement in making rules will help him achieve his goals

- The types of rewards that are especially powerful and when to give them

- If negative reinforcement is as effective as positive reinforcement

- Why a commitment to a behavior modification program can be exhausting—but is worthwhile

Behavior Modification Programs that Work

Trying to get children diagnosed with ADD/ADHD to behave at home and school is the biggest challenge parents confront. They explain, lecture, admonish, nag, criticize, bribe, take away privileges, assign timeouts, and even spank. Too often their child's behavior does not improve or worsens. Aggressive youngsters become increasingly alienated, defiant, and antisocial with each passing year. Compliant children become more upset, depressed, and self-destructive. Parents simply must end the negativity that creates so much upset and frustration. A behavior modification program may provide the solution your family needs.

Teaching Tactics

Six-year-old David was a very bright boy, but his hyperactivity and short attention span kept getting him in trouble at home and school. He could not sit still or keep his hands to himself. Every little thing distracted him. Because he could not concentrate for more than a few minutes at a time, he didn't get much schoolwork done. Soon after he was given an assignment he would notice that his pencil was dull and get up to sharpen it, or he would decide that he was thirsty. En route to the pencil sharpener or water fountain he would strike up a conversation with a classmate, and his teacher would have to tell him to sit down and get to work. After writing his name on his paper he might see that his shoelace was untied. After retying it several times to get it just right, he forgot about his assignment and began carving designs in his pencil with his fingernails or drawing a picture. After just a few months, David's teacher was at her wit's end and David was behind in all subjects. She contacted his parents and said it was critical for the adults to work together to get his behavior on track.

DID YOU KNOW?

When therapists ask children how their parents can get them to do their chores without an argument, youngsters commonly say, "Mom and Dad should ask me nicely instead of yelling at me." If your child misbehaves, ask her what you can do differently and try following her suggestions.

David's teacher and parents developed a behavior improvement plan and carefully explained it to him. The teacher would put a check mark on the board each time he misbehaved. If he got three checks, he would have to stay inside during recess. If he got four checks, the workers at David's after school program would keep him inside during the free play period and have him do his unfinished schoolwork. If David got five checks during the school day, he would not be allowed to watch television or play video games at home that evening.

Progress Can Be Slow

David's behavior improved for a few days, but then it got even worse than before. He dragged his heels when it was time for school in the morning, was more hyperactive and distracted in school, and was more argumentative and oppositional at home. Things came to a head two weeks into the program, when David's parents announced that he would not be able to watch a video with the rest of the family because he had received so many demerits at school that day. The video starred a talking hamster that David had wanted to see. He began yelling that everyone was against him. His parents firmly reprimanded him and said that if he didn't go to his room immediately, he would be grounded for the weekend. David kept yelling, they grounded him, and suddenly David's anger turned into a flood of tears. "I never do anything right," he sobbed. "I'm so bad, I wish I wasn't even born! I wish I would just get hit by a car and die."

Starting Over Might Be the Answer

David's parents were horrified. They called his teacher and told her what had happened. "The program isn't working," they said. "It needs to stop." The teacher pointed out that David was obviously capable of much better behavior since he had improved for a time. "Don't let him manipulate you!" she urged. "You've got to let him know you mean business." What she said sounded completely reasonable but felt terribly wrong. If they went along with her against their better judgment, were they allowing *her* to manipulate them?

The Miracle Cure

By systematically rewarding selected behaviors in a consistent, highly organized fashion and ignoring undesirable behaviors, trainers teach animals to perform amazing feats. They teach dolphins and lions to jump through hoops. Pigeons learn to carry messages to distant locations. Seeing eye dogs master the art of guiding the blind about town without becoming distracted by passing cars, animals, and crowds. In short, animals learn to respond in ways most people never would have thought possible. Psychologists have long recognized that the same straightforward principles and simple procedures work well for animals of all kinds, even human beings!

DID YOU KNOW?

The secret to a successful behavior modification program is to define small, readily obtainable goals and systematically reward each small accomplishment until new habits are formed. Children must be set up to succeed. Failure results when the tasks are too difficult or the rewards insufficiently motivating.

Behavior modification programs are effective for helping children and adults alike eliminate troublesome behaviors, break destructive habits, develop better self-control, and respond in healthier ways. At least, impressive results are commonplace when trained professionals conduct behavior modification programs in controlled environments. When scientists methodically follow carefully designed protocols in laboratories and special education teachers work with students in self-contained classrooms, they typically get excellent results. When ordinary parents and teachers try to carry out behavioral programs at home and school, the results often prove very disappointing.

DID YOU KNOW?

Using rewards to control behavior is often an effective practice. A major benefit is that parents must acknowledge and respond to their child's good behavior. Hence, behavior modification reverses negative communication patterns and strengthens the parent/child relationship.

Many parents are sure that behavior modification won't work for their child, because their past attempts to solve behavior problems by doling out rewards and imposing punishments followed a predictable pattern: most everything they tried worked for a time, but nothing worked for long. Although parents typically conclude that failures mean that their youngster is especially difficult, strong-willed, defiant, or resistant, the real problem usually lies elsewhere. The success of a behavior modification program depends on the adult, not on the child.

The First Step—Define the Problem

The first step in developing a behavior modification program is to create a list of the behaviors you want to eliminate or to increase. Once you make that list, decide what the top two or three problematic behaviors are to work on first. This will keep you and your child from becoming overwhelmed. Examples of behaviors to eliminate are interrupting when someone else is speaking or arguing when told to do homework. Examples of positive behaviors to increase include being in bed by 9:00 p.m. and remaining seated during dinner. Behaviors that are general, vague, or subject to interpretation such as "don't be rude" must be rewritten so that they reflect specific, concrete, observable actions, such as "do not curse," "do not walk out of the room while I am talking to you," and "do not slam the door." Similarly, internal states of mind and attitudes such as "don't be so argumentative" must be rewritten as specific behaviors, such as "do homework when instructed without arguing."

DID YOU KNOW?

Ask your child which behaviors she would like to work on, and add them to the list. You may be surprised to hear her express a desire to learn to control her temper or remember to do her chores. Most children are more motivated to improve than parents think!

Be Precise!

Defining behaviors precisely is a must. Saying that you expect your child to be polite when relatives are visiting really does not tell your youngster what to do. Is she to preface her answers with "Yes, sir," "No, ma'am," and "I'm not sure," instead of mumbling, "Yeah," "Naw," and "I dunno?" Should she say, "Please" when she wants a piggyback ride, "Thank you" when given a present, and "Excuse me" before interrupting a conversation? Or would you just be happy if she would refrain from punching her little cousin, using the sofa as a trampoline, and asking the company to go home so she can watch television? Parents often think that their child knows how to behave properly and is simply being stubborn, lazy, or defiant. Time and again it turns out that the youngster truly does not understand that when mother says, "Do the dishes," she also means "put away the food, wipe the table and counters, and carry out the trash."

Be Positive!

After creating a list of target behaviors to modify, try to eliminate the negatives and replace them with positives by changing the "don'ts" to "do's." Saying that your daughter is not to hit her little brother does not explain what she should do when he takes her toys or taunts her. Telling her to ignore a tormentor may not be realistic and doesn't teach her how to set limits and defend herself.

The Next Step—Recognition and Praise

Children tend to repeat behaviors that are consistently followed by positive consequences. Behavior modification programs use rewards to reinforce desirable behaviors. There are two types of rewards: material rewards and social rewards. Material rewards include toys, treats, outings, privileges, and permissions. Social rewards include hugs, smiles, congratulations, compliments, and kudos. Negative reinforcement, which entails withholding a reward to discourage misbehavior, can also be used but is generally less effective.

Material Rewards

For a behavior modification program to succeed, you must reward your child for a few simple behaviors she can readily accomplish. Then you must reward her every single time until she has thoroughly mastered them before presenting her with more challenging tasks. Since you will be providing many rewards each day, material rewards must necessarily be inexpensive. Items such as stickers, marbles, or trading cards appeal to some children. Many parents give a piece of sugar-less gum or candy, although it is not a good idea to give artificial sweeteners or sugar to youngsters—especially youngsters diagnosed with ADD/ADHD. Outings such as a trip to the mall, city park, or library are popular. Privileges might be getting to play a video game for ten minutes, being allowed to choose the restaurant when the family eats out, or deciding which video the family rents. Some children appreciate permission to do something special, such as being allowed to watch television on a school night and being exempted from a chore.

Tokens Can Add Up to a Prize

Since rewards must be given immediately after a desired behavior occurs, it may be easier to give tokens that can be traded for a bigger prize. However, as everyone who has tried to diet knows, it is hard to remain motivated to work toward a far-off goal. Reward systems only work when children *feel* rewarded. If you discover that your child is not motivated by certain rewards, change them. If she cannot readily earn rewards, make them easier to obtain.

Get Them Involved!

Children should be involved in all phases of a behavior modification program, and their help determining what rewards they can earn and what they must do to get them is important. Explain that you are going to begin rewarding her for good behavior and help her brainstorm a long list of the toys, treats, outings, privileges, and permissions that she would like. Record all of her wishes. You may not be willing to fulfill her heart's desire for a horse by moving Black Beauty into your backyard. But learning that horses mean that much to her may provide clues as to highly motivating rewards.

DOES THIS SOUND LIKE YOUR CHILD?

Solicit your child's input before deciding how many stickers she needs to accumulate in order to earn a trip to the skating rink or to get a new toy. She must view the rewards as worthwhile and believe she can earn them for a behavior modification program to work.

You might consider providing stickers with pictures of horses for her to affix to a chart, renting *The Black Stallion* video, driving to the country so she can pet a horse, letting her take a riding lesson at a stable, going to see a rodeo or horse show, transferring a picture of a horse onto her T-shirt, riding a pony at an amusement park, and helping her arrange to work at a stable.

Social Rewards

Social rewards are interactions that your child enjoys and that are affirming. They can be smiles, hugs, pats on the back, the thumbs up sign, praise, expressions of appreciation, positive acknowledgments, overhearing glowing comments, and spending pleasant time with a parent. Pleasant time can include wrestling, making brownies, planting a garden, turning off the car radio and singing "Row, Row, Row Your Boat," reading a bedtime story together, etc. When asked, children usually choose material rewards over social rewards, but social rewards are powerful and important. They are more meaningful to most children in the long run.

More than a Material Thing

Make it a habit to administer verbal or physical pats on the back whenever you give your youngster a material reward. Some children are indifferent to praise, smiles, and kudos because every other sentence their parent utters is "Good job!" until it sounds like a verbal tic. Youngsters come to regard such glowing comments for what they are: meaningless and empty. Tell your child you love her often, be affectionate, but only praise specific achievements. And when you do, provide a detailed description of the behavior you like: "I'm impressed that you remembered to ask your brother to pass the salt instead of reaching across the table."

Powerful Praise

Combining material and social rewards is especially powerful. Trainers provide material rewards such as scraps of meat to puppies at the outset of training. By combining praise and pats with the food, dogs soon learn to associate the two. Once they make the association, praise alone serves as a reward and keeps their behavior on track. Similarly, children eventually associate the positive feelings about material rewards with their parents' smiles and expressions of pleasure. In time, approval is enough to keep them going.

Small Tasks, Big Rewards

Because a youngster sometimes manages to control his temper or clean his room doesn't mean that he can do either easily. If your child quickly loses interest in earning rewards, you are asking too much of him. Behavior modification programs work because they set children up to succeed. To do that, you must break each target behavior into a series of small tasks that your child can easily manage. Each small success builds confidence and creates the can-do attitude that motivates children to tackle new challenges.

Defining Tasks

Perhaps you want your youngster to clean his room without an argument, but his usual response when told to turn off the television and get started is to ignore you. If you turn off the television and firmly tell him to clean his room, he has a fit and promises to clean it later, but later never comes. Or, he goes to his room but does not work. To solve this problem with a behavior modification program, the first step is to get him to respond when you speak to him, whether he is busy doing something else or is purposely ignoring you. Inform him of this goal, write it on his behavior chart, and specify the reward or the number of tokens he can earn each time he achieves it. Then, when you want to speak with him, go to the room where he is playing, say his name in a normal tone of voice or gently touch his shoulder, and then reward him when he looks up.

Explain the Process, Every Time

As you hand him a token, sticker, or another predetermined reward, say, "I appreciate your stopping what you're doing when I need to talk with you. Thanks." After he has been reinforced a number of times in this way, he'll be better at noticing that you are speaking to him. After he is consistently responding, compliment him on his accomplishment and announce that he is ready for the next challenge, which might be to accompany you to his bedroom without protest when it is time to clean his room. Describe the rewards he will earn for each success. Then, if he willingly accompanies you to the bedroom, reward him even if he doesn't proceed to clean up his room. Help him pick it up or pick it up for him, and reassure him that he will be able to handle that task in time. Don't advance to the next step until he can consistently walk with you to the bedroom and refrain from arguing. When you are sure he has mastered that challenge, describe the next goal: he will pick up his clothes from the floor and put them in the laundry.

Even If It Takes Time . . .

If it takes an entire month for your child to pick up his dirty clothes each evening without an argument, don't get discouraged! Many parents of children diagnosed with ADD/ADHD have to yell to get their attention for years on end. Many adults are too undisciplined to put their dirty clothes in the laundry each day, and the result is arguments with roommates and marital strife. Do not underestimate the importance of small accomplishments!

Negative Reinforcement

Negative reinforcement entails withholding something that a child finds rewarding, such as watching television or playing video games. Ask your child's opinion before deciding what the penalty should be for a particular type of misbehavior, and then watch carefully to see if losing privileges really deters misbehavior and motivates your child to behave correctly. Many children are motivated by negative reinforcement, but others decide they would rather forego television or be grounded than clean their rooms or do homework.

DOES THIS SOUND LIKE YOUR CHILD?

You have probably told your youngster a million times, "If a classmate is bothering you, just ignore her and she'll stop!" Try taking your own advice. If your youngster's behavior is bothering you, ignoring it is often the most effective way to get your child to stop!

Effectiveness Assessment

In general, negative reinforcement is not as effective as positive reinforcement. The exception is withholding attention for misbehavior. Many youngsters misbehave in order to get a reaction from their parents. Even negative attention is better than no attention, so being scolded can actually be more rewarding than being ignored. Many children simply do not know how to get positive attention. Their parents ignore them when they are playing quietly, refuse invitations to play board games, and decline requests to go outside to toss a football. They are chronically stressed and exhausted and only find the wherewithal to respond when a behavior problem compels them to get involved. Behavior modification programs often succeed simply because parents are forced to notice and respond to their child's good behavior.

Sustain Success

There are some limits on what can be taught using behavior modification. Chickens can learn to play the piano but cannot master the art of conversation, or even be induced to utter a single word. You must be realistic when targeting behaviors to change. It is doubtful that you can turn your shy, artistic bookworm into a football star. At the same time, do not underestimate how much your child can ultimately achieve. Through a process called shaping, scientists teach a chicken to play "Twinkle, Twinkle Little Star" on the piano by rewarding it when it accidentally pecks the first note, and by continuing to reward it until the chicken hits the correct note one hundred percent of the time. Then rewards are withheld until the chicken plays the first note and accidentally pecks the second note of the song so that they are played in the correct sequence. The chicken is rewarded until it correctly plays the first two notes every time; then it must play the first three notes to earn a reward. Progress is excruciatingly slow at first but then speeds up dramatically. Chickens learn to play the entire song in short order.

Learners usually understand what they are to do and should be able to earn rewards in short order. Being able to sustain their new behaviors over time is more challenging. Most people can diet or stop smoking for a day or two, but continuing to abstain from fat and cigarettes gets harder rather than easier as time passes. That's because the strain of behaving in unfamiliar ways wears them down.

DID YOU KNOW?

The strain of behaving in new ways is very taxing. Mental exhaustion leads to mistakes. To evaluate whether a behavior modification program is working, consider trends over a period of several weeks. Do not assess progress based on a few exceptionally good or bad days.

Calming Their Own Mind

Although a hyperactive youngster may be capable of sitting still for five minutes at a stretch, doing so requires a tremendous effort. Until your child finds a way to calm his mind, he may well feel as if his nerves are on edge, screaming for him to move about—just as dieters feel that every cell in their body is crying out for food. Your child is likely to require bigger rewards to stay motivated. Until new habits are established, the urge to revert to familiar patterns can be very strong. New behaviors have to be enacted consistently for about three weeks to become habits.

DOES THIS SOUND LIKE YOUR CHILD?

Stress from another problem or difficulty that happens to arise while a behavior modification program is in progress can readily cause a setback. Reverting to old behavior patterns does not mean that no progress has been made. Until new habits develop, lapses are to be expected.

Don't Be Afraid to Interrupt—for Something Good

Do not hold back from giving a reward because your child is playing quietly or is busily doing homework for fear your interruption will create a distraction and end your precious moments of peace. Otherwise, you will quickly revert to the same destructive patterns of nagging your youngster when she does something wrong instead of rewarding her for good behavior, and progress will stall. Until rewarding your youngster for every positive behavior becomes a habit, remaining consistent is not easy. Be patient with yourself, and reward yourself for your successes at carrying out the program. What you must do to succeed is to modify some of your behaviors—perhaps the very same behavior you are trying to get your child to embrace. You must plan ahead to be sure you have enough rewards on hand. You must keep your promise and apply yourself so that you reward your child each and every time he earns one. You must avoid slacking off when you feel stressed, tired, or unmotivated. Behavior modification programs really are a lot of work. But you and your child will reap the rewards for years to come.

When It Starts to Work

After David's parents learned how behavior modification programs were supposed to be run, they understood why the program his teacher had developed was not working. The teacher's negative approach (punishment and negative reinforcement), poorly defined expectations ("behave"), and overly challenging requirements ("sit still and do your work") had set David up for failure. He had learned that his behavior was bad but not how to behave correctly. His parents proposed a new program, and after the teacher agreed to give it a try, they explained it to David. When given an in-class assignment, he was to remain seated and do three problems. Then he was to take his paper to his teacher. If his answers were correct, she would draw a star on his paper. If he made it to her desk and back to his seat without pausing to chat with a classmate, he would get an extra star the next time he approached her with three more completed problems. That way, he wouldn't have to remain seated for very long.

Having Pride in His Work

He was encouraged to do his work and was discouraged from disturbing other students. He would take his papers home to show his parents. Five stars were worth a Pokémon card and ten stars were good for an extra bedtime story. Or he could save them up, and when he got 100 stars, he could use his allowance to buy a hamster.

Within two days, David was doing all of his schoolwork; a week later he felt ready to tackle the challenge of completing five problems before showing his paper to his teacher. Best of all, he was enjoying school and was happier at home. His dream of owning a hamster was still a way off, but his mother had begun checking the want ads for used cages. At the rate David was going, she suspected a fuzzy critter would soon be moving in.

Identify Your Disciplining Approach

How parents discipline and communicate with their child depends on which of the three main parenting approaches they use. Most parents lean in one direction or another rather than using one exclusively.

Permissive: The "Hands-Off Approach." Children make most of their own decisions, and parents limit themselves to suggesting, advising, guiding, and recommending. They assume that happy children will be motivated to behave correctly and believe that youngsters should be allowed to develop in their own way. They focus on building a positive relationship rather than dealing with misbehavior directly.

Flexible Co-Parenting. This is an approach that lets the child be part of the parenting experience. While the parents make most of the decisions, they take their youngsters' opinions into account. They ask for their children's input, listen to their objections, and then make the final decisions. They assume that children need rules and limits and should be taught how to behave correctly, but sometimes even kids have good ideas about how discipline should be carried out. They teach by explaining and enforcing consequences.

Harsh: The Authoritarian Approach. Parents make unilateral decisions. They lay down the rules and communicate by commanding, issuing orders, and by announcing what their youngster must and must not do. They view misbehavior as disobedience and believe a rule-breaker should be punished. To that end, they may take away privileges or spank.

"But This Is How My Mother or Father Did It"

Most parents automatically discipline their child the same way that they were disciplined when growing up. Until about 1955, the authoritative approach (providing clear structure, teaching, and enforcing consequences to improve behavior—more on this later) was in vogue. The permissive approach became popular in the 1960s. For the last twenty years, the authoritative approach has been favored. Most child guidance experts now recommend it. Parenting books, articles, and classes teach parents how to communicate authoritatively and apply the concepts to combat behavior problems. While the approach is sound, you need to consider your child's personal capabilities and individual needs when disciplining. The approach that worked for you may not work with your child. The approach that works for most children may not work for yours. And you need to be flexible. The approach that works sometimes may not have an effect at others.

Different Ways to Handle Discipline

Most children being treated for ADD/ADHD are not psychologically disturbed. Most are not even unhappy, although their parents are suffering greatly. They administer medication because they do not know how to manage a youngster who would rather play than sit still, study, and do chores. Many college-educated parents hope that amphetamines will improve their youngster's study habits to increase her chances of getting into a top college and decrease rowdiness at home. They have talked until they are blue in the face and assigned endless timeouts and other consequences without effect. It is cruel to drug uninspired students and children who are too active for their parents' taste. By comparison, authoritarian parenting methods seem far less harsh, even though they sometimes involve spanking and other punishments.

Bad Behavior and "Getting in Trouble"

Many youngsters steal from their parents because they want money to buy toys and candy. They lie to conceal their misdeeds, not because they fear punishment, but so as not to displease their parents. When asked what will happen if their parents catch them, it is clear that the consequences designed to deter them from misbehaving are unpleasant but ineffective. Most children say they will "just" be grounded, lose television privileges, or have to listen to a lecture. When asked how they manage to behave themselves in certain classrooms or at their father's house but not their mother's, the typical response is that they are afraid of getting in trouble. For some that means having a teacher or parent get mad at them. For others it means having their name put on the chalkboard or being grounded. Still others fear being sent to the principal or being spanked.

DOES THIS SOUND LIKE YOUR CHILD?

Think about this: "Bad" children are unconcerned about hurting others, and are only remorseful when caught. "Naughty" children know the difference between right and wrong. They want to please their parents but want to please themselves, too. They may misbehave when they cannot do both.

Clearly, many children are able to settle down, pay attention, and do a good job on homework and chores when being supervised by someone they consider very strict. Their ADD/ADHD symptoms improve dramatically. Too many are diagnosed with oppositional/defiant disorder as if something were wrong with them. Some are diagnosed with a conduct disorder and viewed as budding criminals. But they are not bad, although they are often very naughty.

Communication Troubles

Permissive parents can have more success getting their youngsters to pay attention by varying how they talk. Instead of following a predictable course from irritated to irate as you repeat instructions and issue reminders, try going from silly to hilarious. Sing your instructions or use the strategy elementary school teachers find so effective: lower your voice to a whisper. When making corrections, speak firmly but do not raise your voice. Explain what your child is to do and why. This is standard practice among Japanese parents, and their children tend to be much more respectful and compliant than the average American youngster. Explaining, "No, you must not touch the candy. It belongs to the store, and candy is not good for you" conveys the rule, teaches that it is wrong to touch items that one is not planning to purchase, and explains why you are declining to buy candy. Adding, "I'll fix you something to eat when we get home" affirms your willingness to meet your child's needs, if not every momentary want and passing desire.

Talk to Your Child!

Toddlers may not understand verbal explanations, and no one likes to be told "no." Regardless of their age, upset children need to be comforted, not shouted at or indulged. A hug and some kind words, such as, "I know you want candy right now. I wish it weren't bad for your teeth" or "It's fun to bang the silverware. You love that noise, don't you?" helps many children to settle down. If your youngster is too angry or upset to accept comfort, try distraction. Have her help you empty the grocery cart in the store or hand her something else to play with in the restaurant. If distraction does not calm her, she may just need to cry or carry on for a bit. Depending on her temperament and how you have dealt with similar misbehavior in the past, the protests may be brief and mild or loud and long. Either way, they will eventually end.

➤ A BETTER PARENTING PRACTICE

If you think you are being too strict with your child, ask him! Ask your child what he thinks he needs in the way of discipline, and how he would handle various situations if given more privileges. If his answers seem sensible, you might want to give them a try.

Don't Get Sidetracked

When your youngster is upset about a rule or chore, it is important to remain focused on the issue at hand. A verbal child can easily sidetrack his parents. For instance, a youngster may complain that too much is expected of him and too little of his brother. Instead of allowing yourself to be diverted, say that you will be glad to discuss other issues when the task at hand is completed. Or, if you are comfortable with using firmer discipline, say that while he is completing the task, you will decide on a consequence to teach respectful behavior or a punishment to convince him that rudeness is unacceptable.

Structure and Consequences: Teaching Tough Lessons
When talking fails, many parents assume they have not used the right words. They keep explaining their position in hopes of finally getting through to their youngster. But some children do not respond well to words. Moreover, some youngsters refuse to participate in family meetings or to abide by the consequences even though they chose them. They would rather sit in timeout, be grounded, or lose privileges. They need more structure and firmer discipline. Their parents may have inadvertently taught them that they need not do as they are told or be responsible. Once destructive patterns have been established they are very difficult to change.

Authoritative Parenting
The authoritative approach does not work for every child all of the time. But it is the most effective parenting method for most children most of the time. It involves providing clear structure, teaching, and enforcing consequences to improve behavior. The consequences used by authoritative parents may be unpleasant but are not intended to punish. Instead, they are carefully designed to "fit the crime," to teach, and to solve a specific behavior problem. For instance, parents may revoke television privileges to ensure that a child who made poor grades has adequate time to devote to his studies. For stealing, the consequence might be requiring a young thief to

apologize to his victim and return the stolen item or compensate him. Money to pay restitution might come from his allowance or be earned from doing chores.

DID YOU KNOW?

Although ADD/ADHD is a psychiatric disorder, the stereotypes about what a psychiatric disorder is do not always apply. For example, few with this diagnosis jump on the furniture, torment their siblings, play with matches, and are cruel to animals because a voice in their head urges them to do bad things. Behavior like this may also stem from curiosity.

If a youngster strongly objects to a rule or consequence, parents should consider his wishes before making a final decision. To communicate that a youngster's desire for candy has been considered, a father might say, "I understand that you want candy, but I will not buy it because it will ruin your appetite for dinner." Alternatively, he could say, "All right, since you missed lunch, I have decided to buy it for you." Either way, the parent makes it clear that he is in charge.

DOES THIS SOUND LIKE YOUR CHILD?

"But what if your mom finds out?" children ask when planning to do something that they know is wrong. "Oh, she'll just get mad and ground me. No big deal," many reply. Others say, "I'd better not. She'll get mad and I'll be grounded." Different things motivate different children.

Hold a Family Meeting

A good time to solicit children's input about family rules, discuss behavior problems, divvy up chores, and determine what consequences will motivate youngsters to comply and cooperate is during a family meeting. Create an agenda, set up a time, and do not try to cover too much at once. For negotiable items, write up agreements and have your youngster sign them. Written contracts can make an amazing difference to a child who is accustomed to being allowed to wriggle out of oral agreements. Agree to disagree when necessary and set up another time to tackle unresolved issues. Or say that you will inform your child as to your decision once you make it.

Harsh Punishment—When Is It Too Much?

Rather than consequences, an authoritarian parent's goal is for her youngster to learn to behave out of fear of being punished. Such a mother may ground her child, assign unpleasant chores, shame, or spank. Some children with ADD/ADHD symptoms seem to need strong displays of parental firmness but do not actually benefit from them. Instead, their disobedience intensifies, and they become sneaky and deceitful or rebel. It is often better to use an authoritative approach for tackling one or two issues at a time and adopt a hands-off approach for everything else.

Physical Punishment—Does It Work?

Even though shaming and spanking are controversial, they are sometimes beneficial. Most parents do both, even while maintaining that such tactics are tantamount to bullying, and are cruel and immoral. Most experts see many abused youngsters and traumatized adults still struggling to recover from childhood traumas inflicted by parents who thought they were merely being strict. It is understandable that they consider harsh methods too dangerous to recommend.

DOES THIS SOUND LIKE YOUR CHILD?

Strong-arm parental methods inspire children to feel afraid, not respectful. Nevertheless, punishment can sometimes motivate them at least to behave respectfully. Too many children order, command, threaten, shame, and punish their parents. Parents do not deserve to be abused, either.

It is interesting to note that in the animal kingdom, adult mammals swipe at misbehaving cubs, pups, and kittens to settle them down or to stop misbehavior, but they do not hurt their young. Many adults maintain that childhood spankings motivated them to behave. Although children dislike spankings, many report that they are sometimes more helpful than lectures and other consequences.

This does not mean you *should* spank your child. In fact, spankings often serve to "rev up" an ADD/ADHD child and thus is counterproductive for controlling behavior. In fact, the American Academy of Pediatrics in their *Guidance for Effective Discipline*, states that "because of the negative consequences of spanking and because it has been demonstrated to be no more effective than other approaches for managing undesired behavior in children, the American Academy of Pediatrics recommends that parents be encouraged and assisted in developing methods other than spanking in response to undesired behavior." Of course, the decision is up to you, but you may do well to adopt other methods of discipline.

Don't Lose Control!

Many parents try to shame their youngsters by humiliating them, which is traumatic and can have serious emotional repercussions. Instead of developing consciences, children become hard and conscienceless. Another argument against spanking is that some parents lose control when spanking. They injure or abuse their child. Even if they do not spank hard, a very sensitive child can be seriously traumatized. Many parents claim they administer spankings to teach their child a lesson but are too out of touch with their own emotions to realize they are hitting out of anger. Because the short-term improvement in behavior is often dramatic, many parents spank too often. The predictable result is that their child's behavior becomes much worse than if they had not been so harsh.

Get His Input

To identify useful disciplining techniques, begin by asking your child what she thinks would help. Avoid punishments that are cruel and abusive. If a child truly feels that he did nothing wrong, a spanking will not convince him otherwise. It will trigger resentment and alienation. To have a positive effect, a youngster must agree that a spanking is warranted. Shaming a child is an attempt to convince him that he misbehaved. If the attempt fails, the result will also be resentment and alienation. To be beneficial, a youngster must have learned something useful. When children perceive their parents as unduly harsh, they are motivated to sneak and lie. Rather than deterring bad behavior, harsh treatment is more likely to prompt a criminal mentality. Teens should never be spanked, and parents need to avoid harshness when disciplining them. If adolescents perceive their parents as unduly harsh, they are likely to flee the house altogether. Many prefer living on the streets to putting up with a tyrannical parent. Many parents are afraid to shame or spank a child diagnosed with ADD/ADHD, because they have been told that he cannot control his hyperactive, inattentive behavior. If that is the case, punishing him is cruel, will be ineffective, and may well create far more serious behavior problems. But some can control themselves and simply choose not to.

Young and Developmentally Delayed Children

A loud, firm "No!" can startle a tot and communicate your displeasure. They can be effective for controlling dangerous behavior, such as running into the street or persistently reaching for a stove burner. If you insist on a swat instead, a toddler will only associate a swat with his action when he is in the midst of misbehaving. If you delay, it will seem as though you are suddenly hitting him for no reason. That can destroy trust and cause serious emotional trauma that leaves lasting scars.

Don't Act out of Anger

If you feel you cannot control your anger, you should delay your angry responses until you are calm. If you don't, you will be more likely to say or do something that you may regret.

A BETTER PARENTING PRACTICE

Try the opposite of what you have been doing. If talking about rules has not worked, use timeouts and other consequences. If imposing consequences has not worked, try explaining the rules and discussing their importance.

Setting Limits

One of the best techniques for disciplining your child is to set limits. This teaches him to know what is expected of him so that he can actually *choose* the right behavior. This helps him develop decision-making skills. When you set limits, explain them to your child, and then tell him what the consequences will be if he does not behave within those limits. Then you must be willing to follow through with what you said. Otherwise, your child will quickly figure out that you do not mean what you say and that the limits have no value at all.

Chapter 9

Dealing with Classmates and Friends

10 Things You Will Learn in This Chapter

- How your child's learning environment might be slowing him down

- Why you might consider homeschooling

- How to work with your child's teacher to find solutions

- How some children are encouraged to move about the classroom during lessons

- That hands-on learning will make more of an impact than any other teaching style

- About a study on the affects of moving and children's educational progress

- How learning disabilities and ADD/ADHD

- About the debate between a child having a "learning disability" or "learning difficulty"

- How to tell when your child requires special attention in the classroom

- How declaring your child as "disabled" may do more harm than good and when to keep him out of special education

Traditional Classroom Settings

Modern textbooks have lots of color pictures, schools have computers, and in some classrooms, students' desks are arranged in a circle instead of rows. Otherwise, education has changed little since the early 1800s, when the goal was to train factory workers. Although the industrial revolution ended a century ago, students still sit all day long, move to bells, and do mindless tasks. Their teacher-foremen try to insert information and then grade students like cuts of meat as they progress through the educational assembly line. On graduation, the prime cuts are transported to premium institutions of higher learning, while the lowest grades work in low-paying jobs or languish in unemployment lines.

New Industry Means New Education Needs?

The high-tech information age needs employees who can think, reason, innovate, make decisions, work in groups, multitask, and cope with ever-changing job duties. The nation's outmoded educational factories need to be retooled, but most efforts at reform involve stricter quality control to lessen the number of defective products rolling into the workplace. Yet their numbers are growing. Some public school teachers are very flexible and work well with students who do not fit the mold. Many innovative private schools can accommodate students with special-needs. Increasing numbers of parents have set up small shops and are homeschooling their youngsters. There are many good options, but parents need to be proactive to ensure that a child with ADD/ADHD symptoms gets a decent education.

Simple Solutions

If your child is having problems at school, the first step is to talk to your youngster to see what *she* thinks would help. Ask what the teacher could do to make it easier for her to understand the lessons, concentrate, and do her work. Next, ask your child's siblings and friends how they see the problem and what they would recommend. They often hear the inside scoop on a teacher's personality, expectations, and classroom problems through the schoolyard grapevine. They are aware of their siblings' or friends' strengths and challenges. Be tactful when broaching the subject so as not to cause embarrassment. Try some general questions such as, "How do you like Mrs. Brown as a teacher?" "Do a lot of the kids have trouble understanding the lessons and doing the work?" and "To be a really great teacher, what should she do differently?" Query your child's previous teachers to find out what worked and what did not.

Working with the Teacher

The next step is to meet with the teacher to conduct a joint search for solutions. Moving a student away from a distracting classmate is often enough to produce a dramatic improvement. Reducing homework loads or providing remedial work can often cure what ails a student. Moving her desk to the front of the room can eliminate the visual distraction of other students. Donning headphones to listen to instrumental music when working on assignments can boost concentration by eliminating distracting sounds.

Kid-Friendly Classrooms

Many children learn better while moving and talking, and a second grade teacher at an exclusive private Dallas school demonstrated the benefits of allowing students to move at will. The rule was that some part of their body had to touch their desk or chair at all times. As long as one finger was on the desktop or a shoe made contact with a chair leg, the students could stand, sit, jump, run in place, or orbit around their seat. When they raised their hands, they could wiggle their fingers, wave their arms, and sway their bodies. Talking was encouraged. When the teacher asked a question, the students shouted, "I know! Pick me!" When they were disappointed that they had not been called on, they could yell, "Shucks!" "But I know the answer!" If a student correctly answered a question, everyone shouted, "Way to go!" or clapped. If the answer was wrong, students made a noise like a gong or a buzzer and called out, "Too bad!" Excitement ran high, and when it was time to work quietly, the students were ready for a break. The teacher never had to stop the lesson to reprimand bored students or remind them to stay on task.

DID YOU KNOW?

Students with attention deficits are often sent to study carrels or their desks are turned to face a blank wall. That helps to reduce distractions, but most concentration problems stem from too little mental stimulation. The trick is to keep students' minds from wandering. If they do, their bodies often follow.

Educators need to be pressed to provide the opportunities for exercise every child needs to remain alert and healthy, and that especially active youngsters require. The trend in recent years has been to eliminate recess and gym to allow more time for academics. A few teachers allow students to go to the back of the classroom to stretch, run in place, or do jumping jacks whenever they need to. Some encourage it. "You look like you need some exercise," a teacher might say when a child is growing restless. "Would it help to stand and stretch?" Students quickly learn to take exercise breaks without having to be prompted.

Different Learning Styles

Many college-educated adults value book-learning and have difficulty comprehending that people can learn in other ways. Although there has been a push in educational circles to present more hands-on lessons, most teachers continue to rely on reading, writing, and listening to lectures. It is no wonder that students who learn best by other methods only like gym, recess, and lunch! Visual students learn best through written language. Pictures, charts, and diagrams help them understand and process information. Auditory students prefer lectures, films, tapes, and learning through dialogue. Kinesthetic students learn best through hands-on activities.

Adapting the Teaching Style

Trying to teach hands-on learners history through lectures is like trying to teach the piano by explaining what to do. Having them read history books is like assigning articles about piano playing. Giving them a written test is like asking them questions about a song to assess their ability to play it. If they can tape interviews with senior citizens, make digital movies, and create exhibits from poster board and clay, they can learn a lot of history and demonstrate how much they learned.

DID YOU KNOW?

The trend is to diagnose "kinesthetic" students with ADD/ADHD. Montessori and Waldorf schools are just what the educational psychologist ordered for hands-on learners. Individualized learning and self-paced instruction are commonly emphasized.

Because kinesthetic students learn best by touch and movement, simply clapping while repeating the multiplication tables can make memorizing them easier. These students grasp mathematical concepts and solve arithmetic problems more quickly by working with sets of specially designed educational blocks. These "manipulatives" come in various sizes, shapes, and colors.

Hands-On Learning

Many students learn more science by taking apart a broken video recorder or dissecting a flower than by listening to lectures and completing worksheets. Educational toys abound, but game-playing is usually a classroom filler activity. Students learn that Park Place and the Boardwalk are expensive properties from endless Monopoly games but never learn which presidents presided over which wars. A good way to teach is to have them invent and play educational games.

DID YOU KNOW?

Moving seriously disrupts children's lives. According to a 2004 National Public Radio report, 35 percent fail their grade in school the year after moving, and 77 percent develop serious behavior problems. Many executives are now declining to relocate, and 83 percent give "family considerations" as the reason.

Special Education and Your Child's Needs

Students with ADD/ADHD symptoms and learning disabilities may simply suffer from a lower tolerance for poor educational practices than their classmates! They do best in educational settings that reflect current wisdom about what every student needs.

Intellectual challenges geared to the student's skill level. Lessons that are too easy are too boring to hold students' attention; lessons that are too hard cause undue frustration and cause students to give up.

Emphasis on understanding and applying concepts. Most teachers place too much emphasis on acquiring information through rote memorization, which many students perceive as useless and tend to forget soon after they are tested on it.

Involvement in setting learning objectives. Some students benefit more from the opportunity to learn a little about many subjects; some do better exploring a single subject in depth.

Opportunities to pursue individual interests. Students are more motivated when they choose the topic they want to learn about. Virtually any topic can be investigated from the standpoint of any school subject. A project on frogs can incorporate reading and writing about them, studying the meaning of frogs in various cultures for social studies, and calculating population growth rates to learn math.

Self-paced learning. Some students need more time to learn the material. They just do. That is not a reflection of how intelligent they are.

Instruction that incorporates the student's preferred learning style. Lessons that engage all of the senses tend to be most effective at reaching the largest number of students.

Involvement in decisions about how they will be graded. Many students learn more from producing a project than from taking a traditional classroom test.

Learning Disabilities

It is common for students diagnosed with ADD/ ADHD to be diagnosed with one or more learning disabilities. Most involve language (especially speaking and understanding what is being said) or a specific academic subject (usually reading or math). A host of educational tests claim to be able to identify learning disabilities, yet many professionals have challenged the whole concept. Most learning difficulties, they maintain, are not disabilities but differences. There is certainly nothing to suggest that the average learning "disabled" student has brain damage. A few generations ago, almost every youngster mastered the basics. The research data suggests some simpler explanations to explain student's academic difficulties, including:

- Disinterest/poor motivation
- Poor tolerance for frustration
- Difficulties concentrating
- Poor persistence and difficulties remaining on task
- Personality differences
- Ineffective teaching
- Nutritional problems
- Sleep deprivation
- Inadequate exercise

Psychologists and educators talk about visual-motor deficits, sensory-integration problems, and dyslexia to explain why so many students do not line up their

numbers in math, spell correctly, write neatly, understand their teacher's explanations, comprehend what
they read, and produce error-free worksheets. A few
generations ago, nearly every sixth-grade student could
read on a sixth-grade level. Now reading deficits have
reached epidemic proportions. Reading problems are
commonly attributed to language-processing and sensory-integration deficits.

The Dyslexia Dilemma

Dyslexia, an especially severe reading problem,
is believed to affect as many as 17 percent of school
children. Recent brain imaging studies have confirmed
that the problems stem from the way sounds (not visual
information) are processed. The problem is blamed on
a hereditary brain malfunction. Yet, instead of reading,
students watch television and play video games. Their
busy parents do not work with them at home. It is ridic-
ulous to say that nearly 20 percent of children cannot
read because a genetic brain problem has disabled them!
For most, the best cure is a healthier lifestyle and better
teaching. Students need to read and play educational
games at home. They need to eat properly, go outside to
play, and get enough sleep so they can apply themselves
in school. They also need to do their homework. With
that said, there is no proof that doing these things will
cure a learning disability or ADD/ADHD.

Services Available to You and Your Child

If regular classroom teachers cannot accommodate your child's educational needs, special education help may be a good option. Special education services may involve going to a special classroom all day, getting extra help in a particular subject for an hour a week, or anything in between. It may mean having a specially trained teacher come to the regular classroom to work with your child. To qualify, a child's ADD/ADHD symptoms must cause significant learning or behavior problems at school. Section 504 of the Individual Education and Development Act legally obligates public schools to ensure that children with a disability have equal access to education. That includes children with "a physical or mental impairment that substantially limits one or more major life activities including learning and behavior." ADD/ADHD falls into this category. Students must receive "appropriate accommodations and modifications" to the regular classroom that is tailored to their individual needs.

Qualifications for Service

To qualify to receive services under Section 504, a student must have a disability that "substantially limits one or more major life functions, including education, learning, and behavior." Only the school can determine if a child qualifies. If you think your child needs special services, the first step is to submit a written request for an evaluation via certified mail to the school. Special education classes are expensive due to the small classroom sizes and advanced degrees of the teachers. Parents may have to be assertive to see that evaluations are handled in a timely manner and that the recommendations are implemented. It is a good idea to request a copy of your school district's policies and procedures for complying with Section 504. It will list your rights and the district's responsibilities. If your complaints are not satisfied, you can call the Office of Civil Rights Hotline of the U.S. Department of Education at (800) 421-3481 for information about how to proceed.

Do *your* homework by talking to other parents about how to get services for your child. IEPs, or individualized education plans, are available if your child has unique needs that cannot be addressed by conventional teaching and classroom methods. These plans allow for modifications that can be made within the educational setting so that your child can manage better.

In the Future ...

With its individualized instruction and self-paced learning, special education can help any student. If the current trend continues, every child may someday qualify. Most students enjoy special education classes and like their teachers. But declaring students disabled can do more harm than good by sending such a negative message about their capabilities. Some students reap more benefits from developing their strengths and talents than from dedicating inordinate amounts of time to struggling to overcome their weaknesses. Fun activities such as gymnastics, Aikido, and piano lessons are good ways to help them develop better balance, coordination, and fine motor skills.

Homeschooling Option

Most people assume that homeschooling requires a stay-at-home parent with a teaching degree and a cooperative, highly motivated child. If you work full time, do not know the first thing about teaching, and have a hard time getting your child to pick up his socks, homeschooling can still be a very good option. Going to school is a source of misery for many students with ADD/ADHD. They learn too little about reading, writing, and arithmetic and too much about their own incompetence. Unless your ADD/ADHD child is a happy camper and is thriving in his current school environment, homeschooling should be investigated.

But just because you consider this option, know that homeschooling your ADD/ADHD child will have a very unique set of challenges. Although the one-on-one approach may be beneficial, it is not going to stop the symptoms that make learning difficult for your child.

Parents as Teachers

Homeschooled preschool children of working parents need childcare since little ones cannot be left alone. But being with a private babysitter in a home can be less stressful than spending long days in a room filled with other tots. If you are concerned about academics, devote thirty minutes to educational activities on weekday evenings and make up the rest of the time on the weekends. A playgroup, swimming lessons, free play at the park, or a couple of half-day sessions at a nursery can provide adequate time to socialize with peers.

To homeschool an elementary student, add an extra bedtime story and practice reading. Play an educational game each evening and review the assignments your child did while you were at work. Make up the rest of the time by sitting down to explain new material on the weekends. If your youngster needs more peer interaction than the neighborhood can provide, enroll him in an after-school program or some extracurricular activities.

DID YOU KNOW?

Most states require parents to file an educational plan. Some districts monitor closely to ensure that compulsory education laws are being observed. Contact your local school district's central administration office or your State Board of Education.

As Your Child Gets Older . . .

By middle school, your student can do assignments while you are at work. He may be able to get most of the individual help he needs online or, if he needs more structure, from a private tutor for a couple of hours. Otherwise, spending thirty minutes to review his work, answer questions, and work out the next day's assignments should be sufficient on weekday evenings. Some public schools are quite hostile to homeschooling; others gladly allow the students to attend part time. If so, parents may arrange for their youngster to attend art, lunch, and P.E. so they can interact with youngsters their own age, or take a foreign language course.

DID YOU KNOW?

You obviously need to do your homework before deciding that homeschooling is for you! Research other parents' experiences by doing an online search for "ADHD homeschool discussion." For articles, materials, and curriculum guides, join the American Homeschool Association by calling (800) 236-3278 or log on to *www.americanhomeschool association.org*.

Since parents cannot teach all of the advanced high school subjects, teens usually get help from Web sites, online tutors, and chat groups. For social outlets, most communities have meetings and activities for parents, students, or both. Teens can attend community events with their parents. Homeschooled students tend to enjoy warmer relationships with their parents and are typically more mature than other children the same age.

Chapter 10

Day-to-Day Parenting Problems and Solutions

10 Things You Will Learn in This Chapter

- How to teach instead of humiliate your child when you are trying to discipline him

- Why some children argue more than others and why they think they can get away with it

- Why you must be specific when you reprimand your child

- How being patient can actually send the wrong message

- How to tell if you are being too strict

- To avoid nagging with the zero-tolerance policy

- Why you need to give your child time to change activities

- How focusing on your child's failures will impede his progress

- How to explain a set of rules and make it stick

- How to find a sensitive balance between criticism and praise

"Pick Up Those Feet!"

"I'll be there in a minute," Shea said when her mother called her to dinner each evening. "Just a second," Shea responded when her father told her it was time to get off the telephone and do her homework. Agreeing to do what they asked her "soon" was Shea's standard response to almost everything. When her parents reminded her a few minutes or hours later of what she had promised, Shea would say, "Sorry, I forgot" or "Yes, I was just on my way" or "As soon as I finish this, I'll do it." Having to continually remind her made them feel like nags. When they finally lost patience and ended up yelling or threatening to ground her, Shea would adopt an indignant, self-righteous tone.

A BETTER PARENTING PRACTICE

Saying, "You should know better!" when your child makes a behavioral blunder is like saying, "You should know better!" when he multiplied the fractions wrong. Telling him that he should know only serves to humiliate him. Your job is to teach what he needs to know.

A Cure for "Soon"

The cure for her foot-dragging was to present Shea with something she wanted to do. She moved with lightning speed when she needed to get ready to go to the mall or when they told her a friend wanted to talk to her and she needed to pick up the telephone. That made her seem hopelessly self-centered. Her parents wanted to set a good example for their daughter by being considerate and respectful of her. They did not expect her to drop whatever she was doing on the spot to do what they wanted. At the same time, it was obvious that Shea was taking advantage of them, and their good example was not teaching her to be considerate and respectful of them—or of her teachers or friends, for that matter.

Limits Are Going to Be Tested

When children persist in misbehaving, their parents often say that it is because they are "testing them" or are "testing the limits." Many therapists also say that persistently misbehaving children are testing their parents to see how much they can get away with. This suggests that youngsters are purposely trying to make things difficult for their parents on the one hand, or are actually begging to be controlled on the other. Both can happen but rarely do. Children continue jumping on the furniture after having been told to stop and do not turn off the television to start their homework when called because what they are doing at the moment is more enjoyable than what their parent is proposing. Their parents' patience may be sorely tested, but such children are not "testing the limits." They are simply ignoring their parent in the hopes that their mother or father will give up, forget, or have a change of heart. Wanting to do as they please does not mean children are lazy or bad; they are just young people following their druthers and having fun.

DOES THIS SOUND LIKE YOUR CHILD

Do not take your child's misbehavior personally.
Just because he is getting to you does not mean
he is out to get you. If you find yourself repeating,
"Quit playing around," your child probably needs
more time to play!

Children learn from experience that they do not have
to do as they are told unless they feel like it—or until
their parent begins counting to ten, dons a particular
expression, or adopts a certain tone of voice. Then they
know there will be an unpleasant scene. Still, many proceed to argue or debate. Even if they inevitably end up
having to comply, they are able to express their feelings
of displeasure by not complying right away. And once
their parent's fit of temper is past, many youngsters
know that they can resume doing as they please. Adults
wear down much faster than children. After having cor-
rected their youngster several times, many parents lack
the energy to tackle the same problem yet again.

When "No" Means "No"

When you ask your child to do you a favor, whether he
consents or not should be up to him. But issuing instructions and then counting to three to give your youngster
time to decide whether or not to obey is a serious mistake. The common practice of issuing the "three strikes
and you're out" threat is a mistake as well, since it effec-
tively allows youngsters to misbehave two more times.
Parents delay taking action in an effort to be flexible, but
there are better ways to cut your child some slack.

Providing additional time or chances for youngsters to comply after correcting them or issuing an instruction sends a confusing message. The end result is that they get a lot more practice doing things wrong than doing things right. Since indulging in forbidden activities and ignoring instructions is in some way rewarding for them, children are reinforced for misbehaving when parents fail to act immediately. When they finally take action, their message shifts from "You should not do that because it is wrong" to "You should not do that when I am really angry and have run out of patience."

DID YOU KNOW?

Saying, "Don't let me catch you doing that again, or you're going to get it," teaches children that their mistake is getting caught! Instead, teach values: "Jumping on furniture ruins it; you are not to destroy property. It is dangerous because you might fall off. You must not do it—not ever."

Communicating the New Plan

Children need to learn to refrain from forbidden behavior altogether. They need to do what their parents tell them the first time an instruction is issued. To teach your youngster, the first step is to discuss how you handled behavior problems and defiance in the past and how you will handle them in the future so that he understands the changes that will take place. Tell your child that in the past you sent some mixed messages by pointing out misbehavior or telling him what you expected, then nagging and giving him second, third, and fourth chances to comply.

Explain Yourself Completely

Explain that you believe he was not trying as hard as he could and that your repeated reminders had not worked to get him to follow rules and instructions. Now that you have realized that motivation and obedience are not the issues; he needs to develop better self-control and self-discipline. Your failure to take action immediately when he broke a rule might have led him to believe that when you lacked the energy to control him, it was OK for him to misbehave or ignore you. Emphasize that misbehaving and ignoring you are definitely *not* acceptable. And whether an adult is present or absent, energetic or tired is not relevant. Each rule exists for a reason, and you will try to do a better job of explaining the rules and the reasons they are important. Your duty as a parent is not to control him; it is to teach him to control himself. Learning to do that will help him immensely at home, school, and in the neighborhood. It will make the rest of his life a lot more pleasant.

A BETTER PARENTING PRACTICE

If you wonder about how strict is too strict, consider this: if the only reason for a rule is a preference ("I always do it that way," "Everybody does it that way," or "I like it that way"), the rule may be unnecessary. Consider other family members' preferences, too.

Every Instruction Comes with an Explanation

List some of the specific household rules your child has trouble with and explain why each is important. Rule number one is that when you issue an instruction, such as announcing that it is time to come to the dinner table, get ready for bed, or to start on homework, etc., he is to comply immediately. That is important because the alternative is for you to nag and get angry. If he is arguing with his brother, blasting the stereo, or interrupting your telephone conversation and you tell him to stop, he is to stop immediately. Otherwise, there will be a consequence designed to teach him better self-control.

Should You Enforce a Zero-Tolerance Policy?

The zero-tolerance policy is not as severe as it sounds. Your youngster does need to learn to follow rules immediately and comply with instructions the first time he is told in order to end the arguments and nagging that make family life so stressful for everyone. But rather than expecting your child to jump to your every command, be flexible by providing advance notice. Announce that dinner will be served in ten minutes so your youngster can finish what he is doing or let you know in advance that he will have difficulty arriving on time. That encourages him to think ahead and bring up problems when there is still time to do something about them.

What You Can Accomplish

Learning to follow instructions without argument and communicating problems before the deadline has arrived will save tremendous time and energy for years to come. But the benefits for your child are even greater. Mastering these critical life skills will serve your child well in school and eventually in the workplace. Teachers and employers expect workers to follow instructions without arguing and to observe deadlines. They need to comply or dedicate themselves to the project of bringing about change—and stamping their feet and swearing is not the way to go about it.

Parental Flexibility

Help your child to prepare for transitions. When it is nearing time for the fun to end at an amusement park or birthday party, or when you want him to be ready to leave the house on time, give the countdown: "We'll be leaving in fifteen minutes . . . in ten minutes . . . in five minutes . . . " That helps your youngster prepare psychologically. If he wants to lodge a protest, he needs to do it in advance, *before* you give the instruction that it is time to leave. When your child objects to an impending deadline, you might or might not decide to extend it. But once you have issued the instruction, "It's time to say good-bye. We are leaving," arguing about staying longer is merely an unproductive way to express anger. If you then allow additional time, your child has succeeded in defying your instruction. That small victory encourages most children to argue louder and longer next time. In many families, arguments about not wanting to leave ensure that virtually every outing starts and ends on a negative note.

Handling Protests

Give advance notice so your child understands that soon it will be time to eat dinner, do homework, etc., and can prepare. If your child proceeds to argue when the final moment arrives, there is no need to say anything. If it is time to leave the house, simply head for the door. Carry a young child or physically steer a tween toward the door. You may need to leave your teenager at home and let her find another way to get to school. If you must carry your child's shoes, hat, and coat so she can put them on in the car, so be it. If your youngster needs to fuss and fume, let her.

▶ DID YOU KNOW?

Transitions are hard for many children with ADD/ADHD. You can help by giving advance notice and by guiding her through the process: "It's time to start putting away the toys . . . time to get your coat . . . time to say goodbye."

Demonstrate by your behavior that she does not have to like rules; she does have to follow them. It takes two to have an argument. If you refuse to participate, there will not be one! And when she does settle down, congratulate her on her accomplishment. Being able to get over being angry about having to follow rules is a big step. Soon she will learn to follow them without so much upset.

Improving Compliance

It is fine to call out or have your child set an alarm so he can prepare to do a chore or leave the house. You do not need to track your child down each time to announce that he has fifteen minutes, then ten minutes, then five minutes remaining. But when you announce that the moment has arrived for him to start the chore or get into the car, it is important to find him and tell him rather than yelling from across the house. In fact, whenever you are issuing instructions, avoid shouting. Most children resent being ordered about and treated in a manner they consider rude. Some children issue instructions of their own by saying, "You do not have to shout!" Others lodge a silent protest by foot-dragging. Be respectful, polite, and considerate. The time to be firm is when your child does not follow an instruction.

Make Your Rules Clear

Outline the rules so your child knows how you expect him to behave before he arrives at a destination, before company arrives, or before he starts doing a chore. To wait until he breaks rules to tell him what he did wrong sets him up to fail. Most children with ADD/ADHD have more than their share of failures as it is. When listing the rules, keep each one short and to the point. For instance, before going into the grocery store, remind your youngster that he is not to run in the aisles, not to swing on the rails, not to beg for toys or candy. You might say that he will be allowed to push the shopping cart as long as he can steer it and not bump into things.

A BETTER PARENTING PRACTICE

How many rules you present depends on your child's age and her current needs. You might focus on teaching a three-year-old just one rule she needs to follow at nursery school and work on it in the car as you drive her there every day for several weeks.

Present rule lists in a straightforward manner. There is no need to announce them as angry edicts or speak in threatening tones. If the response to your rule list is a disgusted, "I know, Mom! Gee—I'm not a baby!" refrain from defending yourself by pointing out all of the rules he broke and all of the babyish things he did when he was in that same situation last time. Instead, be proud: "You're right! You are not a baby." Ask what rules he thinks he has mastered, and what he needs to work on. Before taking your child to soccer, consider the rules he needs to focus on:

- Do what the coach tells you
- Get a schedule of practices and games
- Do not blame others if you miss a goal
- Thank the coach for volunteering his time

Remind Your Child of His Success

After outlining the rules, remind your child of any successes he had the last time he was in that particular setting. Perhaps he only followed one small rule. There is no point in brow-beating your child by listing his failures. However, it is important to note past accomplishments so that he can build on them: "Last time I let you look at the toys while I shopped, and you stayed in that section of the store so I could find you, then you came right away when I called you." Pointing out what he did right reassures him that he can please you, boosts confidence, and pinpoints a concrete success he can build on.

Rules Must Be Followed

Teachers dedicate a lot of time to creating lesson plans before they arrive at school. They consider what they want to teach, and their students' capabilities and readiness for particular types of lessons. Sometimes they put the new lesson on hold and devote time to reviewing old material first. They decide how to present the lesson. They plan what they will say so they can provide explanations in language the students can understand. Teachers also decide what kinds of sample problems to present, whether to go over examples or have students look at them by themselves, and whether to assign homework for additional practice. The same procedures are effective for teaching children to comply with rules. Whether you are taking your three-year-old to daycare or your eleven-year-old to see fireworks at the local park, consider the rules your child is likely to forget and prepare a minilesson to present in the car.

Lesson Plan: "You are not to fight with the other children."

Reasons: You might get hurt. You might hurt another child. Or you might hurt their feelings.

Fighting is not fun. The children won't want to play with you if you fight with them. The teacher will get mad if you fight.

Example: If Mary takes your toy, you need to say, "No, Mary! That is my toy! You have to ask me nicely."

Problem 1: If Mary grabs your doll, what should you say?

Reinforcement: Yes, you say, "Mary, you need to ask me nicely."

Problem 2: If Mary takes your doll and won't give it back, what should you do? Remember that you must not hit her.

Discussion: You could let her keep your doll. Or you could tell her she can only play with it for five minutes and then she has to give it back. Or you could tell the teacher. You could say, "Teacher, Mary took my doll! She won't give it back. Could you please help me?"

Quiz: Pretend I'm Mary. "Andrea, give me that doll! There! I've got your doll, and I'm not giving it back!" What should you do?

Feedback: That's right. You could ask the teacher for help.

The Problems with Punishment
Punishments may help parents vent some of their anger and frustration and can improve children's behavior in

the short run. Hence, punishing misdeeds can be satis-
fying and create the illusion that the efforts to discipline
are working. But research shows that over time, harsh
punishments are associated with worse behavior. That
is undoubtedly because punishment involves controlling through force and intimidation. As youngsters get
older, they become harder to intimidate. Once they are
old enough to escape out a window, it is impossible
to use force to control them. They must be willing to
comply.

Consequences Versus Punishment

For consequences that are designed to correct misbehavior to be of value, they must help children master particular rules. Your youngster may *feel* punished
if he dislikes a consequence, just as it is common for
well-nourished children to *feel* angry and claim they
are being deprived if they want cookies and are only
allowed to have vegetable slices. But that does not mean
their parents are depriving them. Anger is anger; deprivation is deprivation. Since it is easier to avoid or end an
unpleasant scene by handing a child a cookie, and since
enduring tantrums wherein a raging youngster screams
and hurls vegetable slices across the floor is so trying, it
is understandable that parents so often seek to appease
their youngster. But it is important not to lose sight of
what your youngster needs most at such moments: to
learn to control himself. It is natural to hurt when your
child is hurting. But because he feels bad does not mean
you are a bad parent! It may mean that you are a very
good one!

Setting Consequences

The first step to getting your child to comply with your instructions is to discover what needs are being fulfilled by certain persistent problematic behaviors. Next, try to work out alternative ways for your child to meet his needs. Jumping on the furniture may mean your child is angry, bored, or just feels like jumping on the furniture! Find out what's going on and adjust your discipline solution to his needs.

DID YOU KNOW?

Using timeouts are a great way to get your child's attention. Placing him in an area away from attention will help to calm him down. After the appropriate amount of time has passed (a minute for each year of age), calmly explain that his behavior will not be tolerated and then let it go.

Rowdiness before bedtime may signal that your youngster is overtired, so setting an earlier bedtime is often the best consequence. Rowdiness can stem from boredom, too. You might have your child sit down and make a list of ways to entertain himself. Some children become rowdy when they are excited, so meditating for a few minutes can calm them. Some children become rowdy when they are angry with their parent but cannot say what is on their mind. In that case, they may need to sit down and write out their feelings in a letter, pound a pillow to discharge tension, or bring up their complaints in a family therapy session. The hyperactivity that drives rowdiness may be the result of having eaten foods to which the child is sensitive. The consequence may be stricter control of pocket money so that forbidden snacks cannot be purchased at school.

Don't Be So Critical!

Many youngsters with ADD/ADHD are so hard on themselves and so sensitive that criticism of any kind beats them down rather than helping them to improve. Point out an error on a school paper, and they tear it up or suddenly become distracted and cannot finish. Play a game with them, and they cheat or quit the moment their opponent is a tiny bit ahead. Suggest that they did not do a good job cleaning up their bedroom, and they blame someone else or maintain that they are always being picked on. Their egos are simply too fragile to manage any hint that they might be less than perfect. It seems that children would need constructive criticism—how else are they to learn?

Different Tactics

Some parents try pretending that a child's imperfect effort or completely botched job was a great success. They pour on the praise hoping to shore up self-confidence and instill that can-do attitude that causes people to try harder. But phony praise is dishonest. It gives children an overblown view of their competence. Or, because the rest of the world lets them know they are not nearly as wonderful as they had hoped, they lose trust in their parents' accolades. Instead of criticizing on the one hand or showering a very sensitive child with undeserved praise on the other, try giving gentle but honest feedback that instills pride in small accomplishments and points the way to improved performance in the future:

- "You remembered to put away your toys and you cleared your desk. Your room is looking good. Call me when you make your bed, and I'll bring a star to put on your star chart."
- "You got along with your brother for the first eight minutes we were in the car. I think that comes close to setting a record. Soon we'll make it all the way to school without an argument."
- "You did these three homework problems right! Congratulations!"
- "You remembered to hang up your coat! A lot of teenagers can't even do that. I used to lose lots of gloves, but then I realized that if I stuck them in the pockets, they would be there the next time I went out."
- (Speaking loudly enough to be overheard.) "What do I see here? The towels are hung up! And the cap was put back on the toothpaste! If you also start rinsing out the tub after you take baths, the bathroom will be so sparkly, I'll be squinting when I walk in."

When reviewing your youngster's homework assignments, mark the items or the portions of questions he got right with a plus sign or smiley face. Then, if he corrects errors, you can add more marks. When everything is correct, you can marvel over his perfect paper. Similarly, create checklists for what needs to be done when your youngster straightens his room, does the dinner dishes, or handles another chore. Have him call you when he finishes so you can congratulate him on the things he accomplished. Many children with ADD/ADHD symptoms are convinced that they cannot succeed at anything or ever please their parents. List the behaviors you are concerned about, note your youngster's successes, and celebrate by discussing what you liked or appreciated. List areas for improvement under goals, but if you have already addressed misbehavior at the time it happened, do not go over it again.

Target Behavior Checklist

Behavior	Behavior Successes	Goals
Brush your teeth.	Did not argue.	Will not have to be reminded.
Get ready for school.	Was ready on time.	Will remember to take his lunch.
Be considerate.	Helped set the table.	Will not tease the baby.
Be respectful.	Stayed seated during dinner.	Will not make gross sounds.
Control temper.	Said what he was mad about.	Will not slam doors.

Enforce Consequences, See Results

Change, even change for the better, is stressful, Shea's parents learned. When they began tackling her foot-dragging and defiance head-on, her behavior worsened and the power struggles turned into open warfare. "Make me," she said when they sent her to her room. She was sixteen years old, and they realized they could not. They had to work hard to come up with consequences they could enforce.

Kiddy Crimes and Consequences

Problem Behavior	Consequence
Continues arguing when told to stop.	Parents do not respond until child can speak calmly.
Not ready in time for school.	Leave her at home and call the truant officer.
Does not clean room.	Does her own laundry.
Abuses telephone privileges.	No talking on the phone for a week.

Despite the storms that followed, Shea's parents were careful to point out when she was cooperative. When she raged, they comforted her by saying that learning to follow rules would get easier with practice—and that it was critical that she learn. "Soon you'll have a roommate or husband and a job. We are helping you to prepare for adult life." Shea's attitude softened sooner than they had expected, and she became much more pleasant and cooperative. They wished they had started being firmer years ago. But they were trying not to be too hard on themselves, either. They were learning to focus on Shea's successes and not berate her for the things she had handled poorly, and they realized that they needed to be similarly patient with themselves. "Congratulations to us! We're finally getting through to her," Shea's mother told her father. "She's sixteen, and we're finally learning."

Explaining ADD/ADHD to Your Child

Q: What is ADD?
A: ADD stands for attention-deficit disorder. It is the term doctors give to children who have a hard time listening and paying attention.

Q: What kind of problems do people with ADD symptoms have?
A: When students do not listen and pay attention in school, they miss a lot and their grades suffer. Missing parts of conversations can cause them to make unrelated comments that sound strange to others. Children with ADD can have a lot of conflicts if they do not pay attention when their parents speak to them. People with ADD have a hard time organizing their rooms, desks, and notebooks, so they tend to lose and misplace things. They do not naturally keep track of time, which can cause them to be late. Because they tend not to notice and remember details, they make more errors when doing schoolwork and chores.

Q: What can I do about ADD symptoms?
A: For most children, eating a healthier diet, getting enough sleep, and reducing stress improve their concentration and memory, and help them to think clearly. For other children, medication is necessary. For more about different types of medications, see Chapter 5.

Q: Is there anything good about ADD?
A: Many people with ADD like being able to concentrate so deeply on a book, movie, video game, or project that time seems to stop and the rest of the world disappears. When they concentrate so intensely, they can get a lot done. Many children with ADD are able to get the main idea and to see the big picture more easily than people who are careful about details. And many children with ADD are intuitive, which means they often have hunches that turn out to be correct. They know a lot of things without knowing how they know them.

Many children with ADD are especially creative and inventive. Some are drawn to art, music, and poetry. Others are especially fascinated by ideas or inventions. Since people can be creative doing most anything, creative children excel at many different hobbies and jobs. Most people are not very creative, and they admire people who are. At the same time, most people believe it is better to follow directions and instructions than to invent new ways to do things.

Q: What is ADHD?

A: It stands for attention-deficit/hyperactivity disorder. It is the term doctors give to children who are especially active. They may act or talk without pausing to think. Many have a hard time listening and paying attention. Not everyone agrees that ADHD is a disorder. Some think it is a different type of personality that is hard for most people to understand.

Q: What are the symptoms of ADHD?

A: Hyperactive children are restless and have a hard time sitting still. They constantly need to move. They need lots of excitement and action to keep from becoming bored.

Q: What kind of problems do people with ADHD symptoms have?

A: Hyperactive students get into a lot of trouble if they keep getting up from their desks or the dinner table without permission. Most adults get upset when children are rowdy indoors. Rowdiness annoys other children as well, so making and keeping friends can be hard. Unless children with ADHD symptoms pause to think before they do something, they can place themselves in danger. They may run into the street without looking both ways or hurt themselves when playing. They may touch things without first asking permission, which gets them in trouble in stores, upsets family members, and makes other children angry. They blurt comments, annoy others by interrupting their conversations, and hurt their feelings by making thoughtless comments. Boredom is often a big problem for them.

Q: What can I do about ADHD symptoms?
A: Getting more exercise and eating a healthier diet can help with troublesome symptoms. It may be easier to sit still in school, be less rowdy in the house, and to feel less cranky. Although it has not been definitely proven, watching a lot of television and playing a lot of video games may make the symptoms worse. Most people advise children with ADHD symptoms to slow down so they will make fewer mistakes on schoolwork and chores. But the minds of children with ADHD tend to work very quickly. Some children actually concentrate better, make fewer errors, and do better work when they speed up.

Q: Is there anything good about ADHD?
A: Having a lot of energy is great! Energetic people can do a lot. Because their minds work very quickly, children with ADHD may be able to do several things at once and make fast decisions.

Q: Does anybody famous have ADD/ADHD or ADD/ADHD traits?
A: Yes! Many well-known people have traits oftentimes associated with ADD/ADHD. Historical records and biographical accounts suggest that if many successful people were growing up today, they would be diagnosed with ADD/ADHD. Some have achieved enduring fame, including:

Ansel Adams, Photographer
Alexander Graham Bell, Telephone Inventor
Hans Christian Anderson, Author
Ludwig van Beethoven, Composer
Terry Bradshaw, Football Quarterback
George Burns, Actor
Sir Richard Francis Burton, Explorer, Linguist,
Scholar, Writer
Andrew Carnegie, Industrialist
Lewis Carroll, Author
Prince Charles, Prince of England
Cher, Actress/Singer
Agatha Christie, Author
Winston Churchill, Statesman
Bill Cosby, Actor
Tom Cruise, Actor
Harvey Cushing, M.D., Neurosurgeon
Salvador Dali, Artist
Leonardo da Vinci, Inventor, Artist
John Denver, Musician
Walt Disney, Filmmaker, Founder of Disneyland
Thomas Edison, Inventor
Albert Einstein, Physicist
Dwight D. Eisenhower, U.S. President
Malcolm Forbes, Magazine Publisher
Henry Ford, Innovator, Businessman
Benjamin Franklin, Politician, Elder Statesman
Galileo Galilei, Mathematician, Astronomer
Bill Gates, Computer Software Developer, President
of Microsoft

Danny Glover, Actor
Whoopi Goldberg, Actress
George Frideric Handel, Composer
William Randolph Hearst, Newspaper Magnate
Ernest Hemingway, Author
Alfred Hitchcock, Filmmaker
Bruce Jenner, Athlete
Earvin "Magic" Johnson, Athlete
Michael Jordan, Athlete
John F. Kennedy, U.S. President
Jason Kidd, Athlete
Bill Lear, Founder of Learjet
John Lennon, Musician
Jay Leno, Comedian
Frederick Carlton "Carl" Lewis, Athlete
Meriwether Lewis (Lewis and Clark), Explorer
Abraham Lincoln, U.S. President
Wolfgang Amadeus Mozart, Composer
Napoleon Bonaparte, Emperor
Sir Isaac Newton, Scientist, Mathematician
Jack Nicholson, Actor
Michel de Nostradamus, Physician, Prophet
Louis Pasteur, Scientist
General George Patton, Military Officer
Pablo Picasso, Artist
Elvis Presley, Singer
Dan Rather, News Anchor
John D. Rockefeller, Founder of Standard Oil
Company
Nelson Rockefeller, U.S. Vice President
Anna Eleanor Roosevelt, U.S. First Lady

Babe Ruth, Baseball Player
Muhammad Anwar al-Sadat, Nobel Peace Prize
Winner
Will Smith, Rapper, Entertainer
Socrates, Philosopher
Steven Spielberg, Filmmaker
Henry David Thoreau, Author
Leo Tolstoy, Russian Author
Jules Verne, Author
Gen. William C. Westmoreland, Military Officer
Robin Williams, Comedian, Actor
Woodrow Wilson, U.S. President
Walt Whitman, Poet
F. W. Woolworth, Department Store Innovator
Frank Lloyd Wright, Architect
Orville and Wilbur Wright, Airplane Developers
William Wrigley, Jr., Chewing Gum Maker

. . . To name just a few.

Appendix B

Resources

Books

A Symphony in the Brain: The Evolution of the New Brain Wave Biofeedback by Jim Robbins (Grove Press: New York, NY, 2000).

Beyond Ritalin: Facts about Medication and Other Strategies for Helping Children, Adolescents, and Adults with Attention Deficit Disorders by Stephen Garber, Marianne Daniels Garber, and Robyn Freedman Spizman (Villard: New York, NY, 1996).

Driven to Distraction: Recognizing and Coping with Attention Deficit Disorder from Childhood through Adulthood by Edward Hallowell and John Ratey (Simon and Schuster: New York, NY, 1994).

Parenting Children With ADHD: 10 Lessons That Medicine Cannot Teach by J. Vincent Monastra, Ph.D. (APA Lifetools, 2004).

Peer Rejection in Childhood by Steven R. Asher and John D. Coie, editors (Cambridge University Press: New York, NY, 1990).

The Anxiety Cure for Kids: A Guide for Parents by Elizabeth DuPont Spencer, Robert L. DuPont, and Caroline M. DuPont (Wiley: Hoboken, NJ, 2003).

The Gift of ADHD: How to Transform Your Child's Problems Into Strengths by Lara Honos-Webb (New Harbinger Publications, Inc., 2005).

The Gift of ADHD Activity Book: 101 Ways to Turn Your Child's Problems into Strengths by Lara Honos-Webb (New Harbinger Publications, Inc., 2008).

The Survival Guide for Kids with ADD or ADHD by John F. Taylor (Free Spirit Publishing, Inc., 2006).

12 Effective Ways to Help Your ADD/ADHD Child: Drug-Free Alternatives for Attention-Deficit Disorders by Laura J. Stevens (Avery Books: New York, NY, 2000).

The Everything® Homeschooling Book by Sherri Linsenbach (Adams Media: Avon, MA, 2003).

The Everything® Toddler Book, The Everything® Tween Book, and *The Everything® Parenting a Teenager Book* by Linda Sonna, Ph.D. (Adams Media: Avon, MA, 2002, 2003, and 2004).

The Diagnostic and Statistical Manual of Mental Disorders, Fourth Edition, Text Revision (American Psychiatric Association: Washington D.C., 2000).

Pocket Guide for the Textbook of Pharmacotherapy for Child and Adolescent Psychiatric Disorders by David R. Rosenberg, John Holttum, Neal Ryan, and Samuel Gershon (Brunner/Mazel: Washington, D.C., 1998).

PDR Nurse's Drug Handbook by George R. Spratto and Adrienne L. Woods (Delmar Learning: Clifton Park, NY, 2004).

The Feingold Cookbook for Hyperactive Children by Ben F. and Helene S. Feingold (Random House: New York, NY, 1979).

Ritalin Free Kids: Safe and Effective Homeopathic Medicine for ADHD and Other Behavioral and Learning Problems by Judyth Reichenberg-Ullman and Robert Ullman (PrimaPublishing: Roseville, CA, 2000).

Please Understand Me: Character and Temperament Types by David Keirsey and Marilyn Bates (Prometheus Nemesis Book Company: Del Mar, CA, 1978).

ADD/ADHD Behavior-Change Resource Kit: Ready-to-Use Strategies & Activities for Helping Children with Attention Deficit Disorder by Grad L. Flick (Jossey-Bass: San Francisco, CA, 1998).

Without Ritalin: A Natural Approach to ADD by Samuel Berne (Keats Publishing: New York, NY, 2002).

Nurture by Nature by Paul and Barbara Tieger (Little, Brown: New York, NY, 1997).

Web Resources
www.cdc.gov/ncbddd/adhd/
Basic ADD/ADHD information from the Center for Disease Control and Prevention.

www.aap.org/healthtopics/adhd.cfm
Basic ADD/ADHD information from the American
Academy of Pediatrics.

www.meditationcenter.com
Lots of information and tapes to help you teach your
child to meditate.

www.chadd.org
Children and Adults with Attention-Deficit/Hyperac-
tivity Disorder (CHADD)

www.504idea.org
Council of Educators for Students with Disabilities

www.nimh.nih.gov
National Institute of Mental Health

www.ritalinfreekids.com
Information about homeopathic treatments.

www.attengo.com
Information about neuro-cognitive training.

www.schwablearning.org
Information on schooling—a parent's guide to K–12
success.

Videos
Don't Pick on Me! (Sunburst Communications: Pleas-
antville, NY)

Index